BASIC SPOKEN CHINESE
PRACTICE ESSENTIALS

AN INTRODUCTION TO SPEAKING AND LISTENING FOR BEGINNERS

CORNELIUS C. KUBLER & YANG WANG

TUTTLE Publishing

Tokyo | Rutland, Vermont | Singapore

Published by Tuttle Publishing, an imprint of Periplus Editions (HK) Ltd.

www.tuttlepublishing.com

ISBN 978-0-8048-4014-9
Interior design: Anne Bell Carter

Distributed by

North America, Latin America & Europe
Tuttle Publishing
364 Innovation Drive
North Clarendon, VT 05759-9436 U.S.A.
Tel: 1 (802) 773-8930
Fax: 1 (802) 773-6993
info@tuttlepublishing.com
www.tuttlepublishing.com

Japan
Tuttle Publishing
Yaekari Building, 3rd Floor
5-4-12 Osaki
Shinagawa-ku
Tokyo 141 0032
Tel: (81) 3 5437-0171
Fax: (81) 3 5437-0755
sales@tuttle.co.jp
www.tuttle.co.jp

Asia Pacific
Berkeley Books Pte. Ltd.
61 Tai Seng Avenue #02-12
Singapore 534167
Tel: (65) 6280-1330
Fax: (65) 6280-6290
inquiries@periplus.com.sg
www.periplus.com

First edition
14 13 12 11   5 4 3 2 1

Printed in Singapore

A Note to the Learner

When it comes to learning Chinese, practice is essential, of course. This workbook offers you many options for practicing and polishing your language skills, and was designed to be used in conjunction with the book *Basic Spoken Chinese*. However, it may be used to hone speaking skills no matter which book or course you're using to learn Chinese.

There are no Chinese characters to be found here because you don't need characters to learn to speak Chinese. In fact, learning the characters for everything you learn to say is an inefficient way to learn Chinese, one that significantly slows down your progress.

To help you learn to speak and understand Chinese as efficiently as possible, this workbook gives you the Chinese language portions not via characters, but instead through **audio** featuring native speakers (on the accompanying disc). And in the pages of this book, the Chinese is represented in Hanyu Pinyin, the official Chinese romanization system.

- If you wish to learn Chinese reading and writing, which is certainly to be recommended for most learners, you should—together with or after the spoken course—use the companion course **Basic Written Chinese**. It corresponds with *Basic Spoken Chinese* and systematically introduces the highest-frequency characters (simplified and traditional) and words in context in sentences and reading passages as well as in realia such as street signs, notes, and name cards.

- For instructors and those learners with prior knowledge of Chinese characters, a *Basic Spoken Chinese:* **Character Transcription** is also available. It contains transcriptions into simplified and traditional characters of *Basic Spoken Chinese*. Please note that the character transcription is not intended, and should not be used, as the primary vehicle for beginning students to learn reading and writing.

- The *Basic Chinese* **Instructor's Guide** contains detailed suggestions for using these materials as well as communicative exercises for use by instructors in class or by tutors during practice sessions.

附注

《基础中文：听与说》练习册为专门练习口语的教材，因此全书内只列有汉语拼音和英文注释，不使用汉字。学习者宜与配套的光盘以及《基础中文：听与说》一起使用。本练习册亦可作为任何初级中文课程之补充教材，以提高学习者的口语能力。此套中文教材另有《基础中文：读与写》及《基础中文：读与写》练习册，专供读写课使用。《基础中文：听与说》另配有汉字版，将《基础中文：听与说》中所有对话和补充生词的拼音版转为汉字，并分简繁体，供教师和已有汉字基础的学习者参考、使用。此套教材亦包括一张光盘的《基础中文：教师手册》，指导教师如何使用此教材，且提供大量课堂练习，极为实用。

附注

《基礎中文：聽與說》練習冊為專門練習口語的教材，因此全書內只列有漢語拼音和英文注釋，不使用漢字。學習者宜與配套的光盤以及《基礎中文：聽與說》一起使用。本練習冊亦可作為任何初級中文課程之補充教材，以提高學習者的口語能力。此套中文教材另有《基礎中文：讀與寫》及《基礎中文：讀與寫》練習冊，專供讀寫課使用。《基礎中文：聽與說》另配有漢字版，將《基礎中文：聽與說》中所有對話和補充生詞的拼音版轉為漢字，並分簡繁體，供教師和已有漢字基礎的學習者參考、使用。此套教材亦包括一張光盤的《基礎中文：教師手冊》，指導教師如何使用此教材，且提供大量課堂練習，極為實用。

Do you prefer single-sided pages for ease in turning in completed exercises for review & correction?

See the Disc:

Sections **5**, **6**, **7**, and **8** may be printed out in single-sided format.

Contents

Every section includes practice materials for these 10 topics:

Unit 1: Greetings and Useful Phrases

Unit 2: Introductions

Unit 3: Numbers, Dates, Time, and Money (I)

Unit 4: Numbers, Dates, Time, and Money (II)

Unit 5: Locating Persons, Places, and Things

Unit 6: Biographical Information (I)

Unit 7: Biographical Information (II)

Unit 8: Getting Around Beijing (I)

Unit 9: Getting Around Beijing (II)

Unit 10: Weather

Additional Practice Materials in Printable PDF Format: See the Disc!

How to Use These Materials

Basic Spoken Chinese Practice Essentials contains extensive drills and exercises for each unit of the text-book *Basic Spoken Chinese*. The purpose of this workbook is to offer learners various kinds of practice activities for both in- and out-of-class use, so as to enable learners to reinforce and "activize" their learning of the new vocabulary and grammar introduced in the textbook.

New Vocabulary and Grammar Summaries

The first section of the *Practice Essentials* consists of a one-page list of new vocabulary and grammar in each *Basic Spoken Chinese* lesson, from Unit 1, Part 1 through Unit 10, Part 4.

    The lists are divided into a section on "Vocabulary" and a section on "Grammar." In the vocabulary section, each new vocabulary item introduced in the corresponding lesson of the textbook is listed in alphabetical order of the Pinyin with English translation and indication of word class (any Additional Vocabulary is not included). In the grammar section, each new grammar pattern introduced in that part of the textbook is listed, also in alphabetical order, in most cases with one or more examples in Pinyin and English translation.

- We believe these lists of new vocabulary and grammar will be useful for all learners for review purposes. However, learners should ideally not learn new vocabulary or grammar from these lists; instead, they should always try to learn new vocabulary and grammar in the context of the Basic Conversations and Build Ups in the textbook.

- Those learners who are using the *Practice Essentials* to supplement other textbooks and who do not have access to the textbook for *Basic Spoken Chinese*, will want to pay special attention to these lists, since the various drills and exercises in this book assume thorough familiarity with all this material.

The next two sections consist of **drills**. Don't underestimate the value of drills as enabling mechanisms that help you, the learner, to attain the ultimate goal of communicative competency. The drills are useful for improving your pronunciation, developing your fluency, and increasing your confidence in speaking Chinese. Although it's true that some of the drills in this workbook are of necessity fairly mechanical, others are more realistic and communicative, in some cases even incorporating a certain amount of cultural material.

- The drills are best done out of class in self-study mode, either in a language learning laboratory or, working with a computer or your audio player, in some other place of your choosing. If you're learning Chinese in a classroom setting, doing the drills out of class also frees up valuable time with the instructor so that you can focus on those kinds of interactive learning activities for which the instructor's guidance and active participation is essential.

- You should work with the recordings on the accompanying disc as actively as possible, speaking loudly and always thinking of the meaning of what you are hearing and saying.

- If you're learning Chinese on your own, the drills will be especially important for you and, working with the accompanying audio disc, you should try to go through each one several times. In addition, it will be to your benefit to seek out a native-speaking tutor or mentor who can work with you one or two hours a week for additional practice and to answer questions.

Substitution Drills

In the substitution drills, a model sentence is first said for you to repeat. Next, various vocabulary and grammar prompts are given that you're to substitute into the model sentence, creating a related but new sentence.

In the audio portion, after each prompt a pause is provided for the learner to say the new sentence with that substitution. A native speaker then provides a confirmation of the correct sentence, followed by a pause during which you should repeat the correct sentence. An English translation of each sentence is included in the workbook.

- It's most effective to do each drill at least twice: the first time with the workbook open and the second time with the workbook closed.

Transformation and Response Drills

As the name implies, these drills involve transforming one phrase or sentence into another, or responding to a question or other cue. There are also a smaller number of politeness drills, translation drills, and drills involving the conversion of Bejing-style speech to non-Beijing-style speech and vice versa.

In the audio portion, instructions for each drill are given in English before the drill. As with the substitution drills, each of the transformation and response drills is followed by a pause for the learner's response, which is then in turn followed by confirmation of the correct response by a native speaker. A pause then allows you time to repeat the correct sentence. An English translation of each sentence or phrase is included in the workbook.

- Again, it is best to do each drill at least twice—once with the workbook open and once with the workbook closed.

- Though the transformation and response drills are in principle meant to be done by students out of class, some instructors may choose to do some of the drills in class, or some of the drills could be adapted for in-class exercises.

Role Play Exercises

The role play exercises involve conversations between two or more speakers that make use of the new vocabulary, grammar, functions, and situations introduced in the lesson.

There are three to eight role plays for each of the four parts of each unit. In many cases, the role plays are based roughly on the textbook's Basic Conversation but with some of the details changed. Most of the role plays involve two roles (indicated by A and B), with a few involving three roles (A, B, C).

Here in the workbook, the role plays are rendered in English, but they're to be performed in Chinese. The role plays are designed to be done as one of the last activities of each lesson.

- While performing the role plays, you may glance at the English but should try to look up as much as possible when saying the Chinese.

- The role plays should be performed at a fairly rapid clip, so you may wish to practice them in advance (making a few notes is fine, but you should not write out complete translations). The goal isn't laboriously translating word-for-word from English to Chinese but, rather, producing natural Chinese equivalents based on the English cues. The emphasis should be on the *performance* of the role plays. If you find that you're hesitant and choppy in performing a role play, this most likely means you haven't yet attained sufficient mastery of the material.

- If you're learning Chinese in a class, after individual students have performed a role play, the instructor will probably lead the whole class in repeating the lines of the role play one more time together.

- If you're learning Chinese on your own, then the role plays will be especially helpful in giving you practice in using the vocabulary and grammar of the lesson in new combinations. By playing all the roles in a role play exercise, you as an independent learner stand to gain extra benefits for your language skills, enhancing your fluency and becoming flexible in swiftly switching perspectives. Of course, if you're learning with a friend or have access to a native-speaking tutor, then each of you could take one role.

Listening Comprehension Exercises

The listening comprehension exercises involve conversations or monologues which are available on the accompanying disc only, since it is *listening* that we want to practice, not reading.[1] There are two listening passages for each lesson, each approximately the same length as the basic conversations, that is, about 6 to 12 lines total. To provide additional practice in listening comprehension, the passages reuse, in new contexts, the new vocabulary (including the Supplementary Vocabulary) and grammar of the current and previous lessons.

Each listening passage is followed by two to four multiple choice questions on the content of the passage. Based on the recorded passages, you should circle the best response—(A), (B), or (C)—to each of the questions that follows.

- While you work on the listening comprehension exercises, feel free to listen to each passage as many times as needed.

- In a classroom setting, the listening comprehension exercises are best done as homework which students hand in the next day for the instructor to correct, grade, and return. After they have been corrected and returned to students, they can be inserted by the student into a binder for future reference.

- Independent learners will also find the listening comprehension exercises helpful for practice in comprehending new combinations of words and grammar patterns; if they have questions, they can ask a tutor or Chinese friend. It may also be useful to obtain the *Instructor's Guide*, since along with the scripts for the listening comprehension exercises it also includes the correct answers.

Dictation Exercises

The dictation exercises provide practice in listening to and transcribing in Pinyin romanization the sounds of Mandarin, as well as listening comprehension practice involving the classroom expressions, numbers, ages, money amounts, clock times, amounts of time, and dates (days of the week, days of the month, months, and years).

Dictation exercises are included only for some of the lessons in the textbook. The lesson in the textbook that a given dictation exercise is designed to accompany is indicated.

The dictation exercises provide all learners, independent or class-based alike, with additional practice to reinforce the content of the lesson. If you're learning Chinese in a classroom setting, your

---

1. Complete scripts of the listening comprehension exercises in Chinese characters are available in the *Instructor's Guide*, which also includes other exercises for in-class use.

instructor may suggest that you do the dictation exercises as homework to reinforce what's been covered in class.

- Like the listening comprehension exercises, the dictation exercises are based on audio recordings by native speakers that are available only on the accompanying disc.[2] Instructions are given in English at the beginning of each exercise.

- You may listen to each dictation exercise as many times as you wish.

- Also like the listening comprehension exercises, the dictation exercises may be removed from the workbook for correction by the instructor, then may be kept in a binder for reference.

Translation Exercises

The purpose of the translation exercises is to provide you with additional practice in using the grammar patterns and important vocabulary of the unit and to serve as a check of mastery over the material. Completing the translation exercises will be helpful to students in reviewing for the unit tests.

It is recommended that the classroom instructor correct and return the translation exercises to students before the test on the corresponding unit, so that any remaining problems can be identified and addressed in a timely manner. Students should carefully study the instructor's corrections, making sure they understand why any errors occurred, and file the corrected exercises for later reference.

The translation exercises come in two different sets. The first set of translation exercises consists of five sentences *for each of the four Parts* or lessons of each Unit in the textbook, while the second set of translation exercises consists of ten sentences *for each complete Unit* of the textbook. Instructors can decide whether the students in their classes should complete both sets or only one of the two sets. Independent learners would profit from doing both sets of translation exercises and can read out their translations to a tutor or native-speaking friend for correction and comments.

- The sentences should be translated into Pinyin romanization with correct tone marks in the blank space that has been left under each sentence.

- The English in the translation exercises is in some places purposely somewhat stilted, so as to guide the student toward the correct Chinese translation.

- In certain cases, additional instructions have been added in parentheses within or after the English sentence, for example, to be polite or to use or not use certain words or patterns.

- If you've forgotten the Chinese equivalent for an English word or grammar pattern, you can consult the English-Chinese Glossary, Chinese-English Glossary, or Index of Grammatical and Cultural Topics in the back of the *Basic Spoken Chinese* textbook.

---

2. Scripts of the dictation exercises are also included in the *Instructor's Guide.*

Abbreviations

Word Classes*

A	Adverb
AT	Attributive
AV	Auxiliary Verb
BF	Bound Form
CJ	Conjunction
CV	Coverb
EV	Equative Verb
EX	Expression
I	Interjection
IE	Idiomatic Expression
L	Localizer
M	Measure
MA	Moveable Adverb
N	Noun
NU	Number
P	Particle
PH	Phrase
PR	Pronoun
PT	Pattern
PV	Postverb
PW	Place Word
QW	Question Word
RC	Resultative Compound
RE	Resultative Ending
SN	Surname
SP	Specifier
SV	Stative Verb
TW	Time Word
V	Verb
VO	Verb-Object Compound

Other Abbreviations and Symbols

(B)	Beijing
(T)	Taipei
lit.	literally
SV	Supplementary Vocabulary
AV	Additional Vocabulary
*	(indicates that what follows is incorrect
/	(separates alternate forms)

* For explanations of the word classes, see the section "Word Classes of Spoken Chinese" in *Basic Spoken Chinese*.

1. New Vocabulary and Grammar Summaries

Unit 1, Part 1: New Vocabulary and Grammar

Vocabulary

a	(softens sentence) [P]
bàn	take care of, do [V]
dào	to [CV]
huí	go back to [V]
Kē	Ke [SN]
năr	where [QW]
ne	and how about, and what about [P]
nĭ	you [PN]
nĭ hăo	hi, how are you? [IE]
qù	go [V]
shì(r)	matter [N]
shítáng	cafeteria [PW]
sùshè	dormitory [PW]
túshūguăn	library [PW]
Wáng	Wang [SN]
wŏ	I [PN]
yĕ	also, too [A]
yìdiăn(r)	a little [N]

Grammar

A as final particle to soften questions, greetings, and exclamations: **Nĭ dào năr qù a?** "And where might you be going?"

DÀO...QÙ "go to...": **Wáng Jīngshēng dào năr qù?** "Where is Jingsheng Wang going?"

Name + Greeting: **Wáng Jīngshēng, nĭ hăo!** "Jingsheng Wang, how are you?"

Names: **Wáng Jīngshēng** "Jingsheng Wang"

NE as final particle to abbreviate questions: **Wŏ qù shítáng. Nĭ ne?** "I'm going to the dining hall. And what about you?"

QÙ + Place word to indicate "go to a certain place": **Wŏ qù túshūguăn.** "I'm going to the library."

QÙ + Verb to indicate purpose: **Wŏ qù túshūguăn bàn yìdiănr shì.** "I'm going to the library to take care of something."

Question Word Questions: **Nĭ dào năr qù?** "Where are you going?"

· ·

Unit 1, Part 2: New Vocabulary and Grammar

Vocabulary

àirén	spouse [N]
bàba	dad [N]
dōu	all, both [A]
hái	still [A]
háizi	child [N]
hǎo jiǔ bú jiànle	long time no see [IE]
hǎo	be good [SV]
hěn	very [A]
le	(indicates changed status or situation) [P]
lèi	be tired [SV]
ma	(indicates questions) [P]
māma	mom [N]
máng	be busy [SV]
tā	he, she [PN]
tāmen	they [PN]
xiān	first [A]
xièxie	thank you [IE]
xíng	be O.K. [V]
yǒu	have [V]
zàijiàn	goodbye [IE]
zěmmeyàng	how, in what way [QW]
Zhào	Zhao [SN]
zǒu	depart [V]

Grammar

MA to transform statements into questions: **Tāmen yě qù shítáng ma?** "Are they going to the dining hall, too?"

Stative Verb Sentences: **Wǒ hěn lèi.** "I'm tired."

Unmarked coordination: **nǐ àirén, háizi** "your spouse and children"

Unit 1, Part 3: New Vocabulary and Grammar

Vocabulary

ǎi	be short [SV]
bù	not [A]
-de	(in **tǐng...-de** "quite, very") [P]
èi	hey, hi [I]
Gāo	Gao [SN]
gāo	be tall [SV]
gōngzuò	work [N]
Hé	He [SN]
jǐnzhāng	be intense [SV]
kéyi	be O.K. [SV]
kùn	be sleepy [SV]
lǎo	be old [SV]
nán	be difficult [SV]
róngyi	be easy [SV]
shì	be [EQ]
tài	too, excessively [A]
tǐng	quite, very [A]
xiǎo	be small [SV]
xuéxí	study, studies [N]
yàngzi	way [N]
Zhōngwén	Chinese language [N]
zuìjìn	recently [TW]

Grammar

Affirmative-Negative Questions: **Zhōngwén nán bu nán?** "Is Chinese hard?"

BÙ to negate verbs: **bù máng** "not be busy," **bù huí sùshè** "not go back to the dormitory"

LǍO and **XIǍO** before monosyllabic surnames: **Lǎo Gāo** "Old Gao," **Xiǎo Wáng** "Little Wang"

Stative Verbs before nouns as adjectives: **lǎo yàngzi** "old way," **hǎo háizi** "good child," **xiǎo shìr** "small matter"

TǏNG...-DE: **tǐng jǐnzhāngde** "quite intense," **tǐng róngyide** "quite easy"

Tone change of **BÙ** to **BÚ** before Tone Four syllables: **bù + qù → bú qù**

Topic-comment construction: **Nǐ gōngzuò máng bu máng?** "Is your work busy or not busy?"

Vocative Expressions: **Xiǎo Liú!** "Little Liu!," **Bàba!** "Dad!"

· ·

Unit 1, Part 4: New Vocabulary and Grammar

Vocabulary

bú kèqi	you're welcome [IE]
děi	must [AV]
huānyíng	welcome [IE]
jìn	enter [V]
lǎoshī	teacher [N]
Lǐ	Li [SN]
Lín	Lin [SN]
màn zǒu	take care [IE]
méi yìsi	not be interesting [PH]
nǐmen	you (plural) [PN]
nín	you (polite) [PN]
qǐng jìn	please come in [IE]
qǐng zuò	please sit down [IE]
qǐng	please [IE]
tàitai	Mrs. [N]
wǒmen	we [PN]
xiānsheng	Mr. [N]
xiáojie	Miss [N]
Xiè	Xie [SN]
xièxie	thank [V]
yǒu yìsi	be interesting [PH]
zuò	sit [V]

Grammar

Imperatives: **Qǐng nín dào túshūguǎn qù.** "Please go to the library."

LE to indicate a changed situation: **Nǐ māma hǎole ma?** "Has your mom gotten well?," **Wǒ bú qùle.** "I'm no longer going."

Pronouns: **wǒ, nǐ, nín, tā, wǒmen, nǐmen, tāmen**

Titles: **Wáng Xiānsheng** "Mr. Wang," **Lǐ Tàitai** "Mrs. Li," **Wáng Xiáojie** "Miss/Ms. Wang," **Lín Lǎoshī** "Teacher Lin"

Unit 2, Part 1: New Vocabulary and Grammar

Vocabulary

Bái	Bai (lit. "white") [SN]
Chén	Chen [SN]
Huáyì Měiguo rén	Chinese-American [PH]
Huáyì	person of Chinese descent [N]
Jiā'nádà	Canada [PW]
jiào	be called or named [EQ]
kěshi	but [MA]
Mǎ	Ma (lit. "horse") [SN]
Mǎláixīyà	Malaysia [PW]
Měiguo	America [PW]
míngzi	name [N]
nèi-	that [SP]
něi-	which [QW]
něiguó	which country [QW]
qǐng wèn	"excuse me," "may I ask" [IE]
rén	person [N]
Rìběn	Japan [PW]
shémme	what [QW]
Táiwān	Taiwan [PW]
tóngxué	classmate [N]
wèi	(polite measure for people) [M]
wèn	ask [V]
Xībānyá	Spain [PW]
Xīnjiāpō	Singapore [PW]
zhèi-	this [SP]
Zhōngguo	China [PW]

Grammar

JIÀO in equative verb sentences: **Wǒ jiào Bái Jiéruì.** "My name is Bai Jierui." **Nǐ jiào shémme míngzi?** "What's your name?"

Nationalities: **Měiguo rén** "American," **Zhōngguo rén** "Chinese," etc.

SHÌ in equative verb sentences: **Wǒ shi Měiguo rén.** "I am (an) American."

ZHÈI- and **NÈI-** as specifiers with the polite measure **WÈI**: **zhèiwèi lǎoshī** "this teacher," **nèiwèi tóngxué** "that classmate"

Unit 2, Part 2: New Vocabulary and Grammar

Vocabulary

bié	don't [AV]
búyào	don't [AV]
chēnghu	address [V]
-de	(indicates possession) [P]
gāoxìng	be happy [SV]
gěi	for [CV]
hǎo	"all right," "O.K." [IE]
huānyíng	welcome [V]
jiào	call (someone a name) [V]
jièshao	introduce [V]
lái	come [V]
nà	in that case [CJ]
nà	that [PN]
ò	"oh" [I]
rènshi	be acquainted with, know [V]
shéi	who, whom [QW]
tóngwū(r)	roommate [N]
xīn	be new [SV]
yīnggāi	should [AV]
zěmme	how [QW]
zhè	this [PN]
zhèmme	like this, in this way, so [A]

Grammar

BIÉ or **BÚYÀO** to indicate negative imperative: **Qǐng nǐ bié qù!** "Please don't go!" **Búyào jiào wǒ Lǎo Wáng!** "Don't call me old Wang!"

DÀO...LÁI: **Qǐng nǐ dào túshūguǎn lái.** "Please come to the library."

-DE to indicate possession: **wǒde gōngzuò** "my work," **nǐde xīn tóngxué** "your new classmate"

...HǍOLE: **Nǐ hái shi jiào wǒ Xiǎo Chén hǎole.** "It would be better if you called me Little Chen."

YÍXIÀ(R) after verbs to make them less abrupt: **jièshao yixiar** "introduce," **lái yixia** "come," **wèn yixia** "ask"

ZHÈ "this" and **NÀ** "that" as pronoun subjects: **Zhè shi Wáng Àihuá, zhè shi Chén Lì** "This is Wang Aihua, this is Chen Li," **Nà shi shéi?** "Who is that?"

Unit 2, Part 3: New Vocabulary and Grammar

Vocabulary

ba	(indicates supposition) [P]
dānwèi	work unit, organization [PW]
dàshǐguǎn	embassy [PW]
dàxué	university, college [PW]
ge	(general measure) [M]
gōngsī	company, firm [PW]
gōngzuò	work [V]
guìxìng	"what's your honorable surname?" [IE]
jiā	(for companies, factories) [M]
nǚshì	madam, lady [N]
tàitai	wife [N]
tóngshì	colleague [N]
wàijiāobù	foreign ministry [PW]
Wú	Wu [SN]
Xiānggǎng	Hong Kong [PW]
xiānsheng	husband [N]
xiàozhǎng	head of a school [N]
xìng	be surnamed [EQ]
xuéxí	learn, study [V]
yī	one, a [NU]
zài	be located at, at [CV]

Grammar

BA to indicate supposition: **Tā shi Yīngguo rén ba** "I suppose she's English." **Nǐ lèile ba?** "You must be tired?"

XÌNG in equative verb sentences: **Wǒ xìng Zhāng.** "My last name is Zhang." **Nǐ xìng shémme?** "What's your last name?"

Unit 2, Part 4: New Vocabulary and Grammar

Vocabulary

à	"oh" [I]
cuò	be wrong [SV]
-cuò	wrong [RE]
dài	take along, bring [V]
-de	(indicates that what precedes describes what follows) [P]
gǎo	get, do [V]
gǎocuò	get or do something wrong [RC]
gēn	and [CJ]
Hóu	Hou [SN]
jīnglǐ	manager [N]
-le	(indicates completed action) [P]
Luó	Luo [SN]
màoyì gōngsī	trading company [PH]
màoyì	trade [N]
méi guānxi	"never mind" [IE]
méi	(indicates past negative of action verbs) [AV]
míngpiàn	name card, business card [N]
Shī	Shi [SN]
tàitai	married woman, lady [N]
xiānsheng	gentleman [N]
xiáojie	young lady [N]
Yīngguo	England [PW]
Zhōng-Měi	Sino-American [AT]
zǒngjīnglǐ	general manager [N]

Grammar

BÙ DŌU vs. **DŌU BÙ**: **Wǒmen bù dōu shi Měiguo rén.** "We are not all Americans." **Wǒmen dōu bú shi Měiguo rén.** "None of us is American."

-DE to indicate that what precedes describes what follows: **Zhōng-Měi Màoyì Gōngsīde Shī Xiáojie** "Ms. Shi from Sino-American Trading Company"

-LE to indicate completed action: **Wǒ gǎocuòle.** "I got it wrong."

MÉI to indicate past negative of action verbs: **Tāmen méi lái.** "They didn't come."

MÉI DŌU vs. **DŌU MÉI**: **Tāmen méi dōu qù.** "They didn't all go." **Tāmen dōu méi qù.** "None of them went."

Unit 3, Part 1: New Vocabulary and Grammar

Vocabulary

bā	eight [NU]
bān	class [N]
bàn(r)	half [NU]
Déguo	Germany [PW]
èr	two [NU]
Fǎguo	France [PW]
jǐ-	how many [QW]
jiǔ	nine [NU]
liǎng-	two [NU]
liù	six [NU]
nánde	man, male [N]
nánlǎoshī	male teacher [N]
nánshēng	male student [N]
nǚde	woman, female [N]
nǚlǎoshī	female teacher [N]
nǚshēng	female student [N]
qī	seven [NU]
sān	three [NU]
shí	ten [NU]
sì	four [NU]
wǔ	five [NU]
yígòng	in all [A]
yǒu	there is, there are [V]

Grammar

Numbers from one to ten

Place Word + **YǑU** + Noun Phrase to indicate existence: **Bānshang yǒu shíge tóngxué.** "In the class there are ten classmates."

Unit 3, Part 2: New Vocabulary and Grammar

Vocabulary

ài	love; like [V]
cāi	guess [V]
dà	be big; old (of people) [SV]
dìdi	younger brother [N]
duì	be correct [SV]
duō	how [QW]
fùqin	father [N]
gēge	older brother [N]
jiějie	older sister [N]
jīnnián	this year [TW]
jiù	then [A]
kàn	look, see [V]
kě'ài	be loveable, cute [SV]
mèimei	younger sister [N]
méiyou	not have; there is/are not [V]
mǔqīn	mother [N]
niánji	age [N]
shàng-	last [SP]
suì	year of age [M]
xià-	next [SP]
xiǎng	think [V]
yuè	month [N]

Grammar

Age: **Nǐ duō dà niánji le?** "How old are you?"; **Nǐ jǐsuì le?** "How old are you?" (of children); **Wǒ jīnnián shíbāsuì le.** "I'm eighteen years old."

LE to indicate anticipated change in a situation: **Tā xiàge yuè jiù jiǔsuì le** "Next month she will be nine years old."

MÉIYOU "not have; there is not/there are not" as the negative of YǑU: **Wǒ méiyou gēge.** "I don't have (any) brothers."

Numbers from 11 to 99 with **SHÍ**

Reduplicated monosyllabic verbs + **KÀN**: **xiángxiang kàn** "try and think"

Tag Questions: **Zhè shi nǐ mèimei, duì bu duì?** "This is your younger sister, right?"; **Zhè shi nǐ dìdi, shì bu shì?** "This is your younger brother, isn't it?"

Unit 3, Part 3: New Vocabulary and Grammar

Vocabulary

a	(indicates suggestions) [P]
-bǎi	hundred [NU]
bēibāo	knapsack, backpack [N]
bēizi	cup [N]
dàizi	bag [N]
duōshǎo	how much, how many [QW]
fēn	penny [M]
gōngshìbāo	briefcase, attache case [N]
guì	be expensive [SV]
jiā	add; plus [V]
jiǎn	subtract; minus [V]
kuài	dollar (monetary unit) [M]
líng	zero [NU]
mǎi	buy [V]
mài	sell [V]
máo	ten cents, dime [M]
piányi	be cheap [SV]
-qiān	thousand [NU]
qián	money [N]
yào	want, need, cost, take [V]
yī	one [NU]
yò	"gosh," "wow" [I]
zhǐ	only [A]

Grammar

BA to indicate suggestions: **Nín kàn ba.** "Why don't you take a look?"

LE after **TÀI** in affirmative sentences: **tài guìle** "too expensive"

Monetary system: **liùkuài wǔmáo jiǔfēn qián** "six dollars and fifty-nine cents"

Numbers from 100 to 999 with **-BǍI** "hundred"

Numbers from 1,000 to 9,999 with **-QIĀN** "thousand"

Reduplication of verbs: **kàn** → **kànkan** "take a look"

YÀO to indicate price: **Nèige bēizi yào sānkuài wǔ.** "That cup costs three fifty."

ZHÈIGE "this/this one" and **NÈIGE** "that/that one"

Unit 3, Part 4: New Vocabulary and Grammar

Vocabulary

chà	lack [V]
chàbuduō	almost, about [MA]
cháng	be long [SV]
chē	vehicle (car, cab, bus, bicycle) [N]
dào	arrive, reach [V]
diǎn	o'clock, hour [M]
fēn	minute [M]
huǒ	fire [N]
huǒchē	train [N]
-jí	reach a goal in time [RE]
kāi	depart (of a train, bus, ship) [V]
kè	quarter of an hour [M]
kǒngpà	"I'm afraid that"; probably [MA]
láibují	not have enough time [RC]
nèmme	then, in that case, well [CJ]
shíjiān	time [N]
tàng	(for runs by trains, buses) [M]
Tiānjīn	Tianjin [PW]
xiànzài	now [TW]
yǐjīng	already [A]
zài	again [A]
zhōng	clock, o'clock; bell [N]
zhōngtóu	hour [N]
zuò	travel by, take [V]

Grammar

Clock times: **liǎngdiǎn sānshibāfēn zhōng** "2:38"

-DE following long phrases to indicate modification: **dào Tiānjīnde huǒchē** "the trains that go to Tianjin"

-DE to create nominal phrases: **shídiǎn bànde** "the 10:30 one," **wǒ mǎide** "the ones I bought"

Number of hours: **sān'ge zhōngtóu** "three hours"

Time when before the verb: **Wǒ bādiǎn zhōng qù.** "I go at eight o'clock."

Unit 4, Part 1: New Vocabulary and Grammar

Vocabulary

guān	close [V]
guānmén	close a door, close [VO]
kāi	open [V]
kāimén	open a door, open [VO]
lǐbài	week [N]
měi-	each, every [SP]
mén(r)	door, gate [N]
náli	"not at all" [IE]
píngcháng	usually, ordinarily [MA]
qǐchuáng	get up from bed, rise [VO]
shàngwǔ	morning, A.M. [TW]
shíyàn	experiment [N]
shíyànshì	laboratory [N]
shuì	sleep [V]
shuìjiào	sleep, go to bed [VO]
tiān	day [M]
wǎnshang	in the evening [TW]
xiàwǔ	afternoon, P.M. [TW]
xīngqī	week [N]
xiūxi	rest, take time off [V]
yǔyán shíyànshì	language lab [PH]
yǔyán	language [N]
zǎoshang	in the morning [TW]

Grammar

Days of the week: **xīngqīyī** OR **lǐbàiyī** "Monday," **xīngqī'èr** OR **lǐbài'èr** "Tuesday," **xīngqīsān** OR **lǐbàisān** "Wednesday," **xīngqīsì** OR **lǐbàisì** "Thursday," **xīngqīwǔ** OR **lǐbàiwǔ** "Friday," **xīngqīliù** OR **lǐbàiliù** "Saturday," **xīngqītiān** OR **xīngqīrì** OR **lǐbàitiān** OR **lǐbàirì** "Sunday," **xīngqījǐ** OR **lǐbàijǐ** "which day of the week?"

TIĀN as measure meaning "day": **yìtiān** "one day," **liǎngtiān** "two days," **jǐtiān** "how many days?," **měitiān** "every day"

Time spent after the verb: **Yǔyán shíyànshì xīngqīliù kāi bàntiān.** "On Saturday the language lab is open for half the day."

Unit 4, Part 2: New Vocabulary and Grammar

Vocabulary

chūshēng	be born [V]
děng	wait, wait for [V]
dìzhǐ	address [N]
dōng	east [L]
duàn	section [M]
gōng	bow (the weapon) [N]
hào	day of the month; number (in addresses, sizes) [M]
hépíng	peace [N]
jīnnián	this year [TW]
jīntiān	today [TW]
jiù	precisely, exactly [A]
lóu	floor (of a building) [N]
míngnián	next year [TW]
míngtiān	tomorrow [TW]
Mínguó	the Republic (of China) [TW]
nián	year [M]
-nòng	alley [BF]
qùnián	last year [TW]
shēngrì	birthday [N]
wénhuà	culture [N]
-xiàng	lane [BF]
Zhāng	Zhang [SN]
zuótiān	yesterday [TW]

Grammar

Addresses: **Zhōngguo Guǎngdōng Guǎngzhōu Zhōngshān Lù wǔhào sānlóu** "3rd floor, Number 5, Zhong Shan Road, Guangzhou, China"

Dates: **èr-líng-líng-wǔ nián shíyīyuè èrhào xīngqīyī** "Monday, November 2, 2005"

Days of the month with **HÀO**: **wǔhào** "the fifth," **jǐhào** "which day of the month?"

Floors of buildings with **LÓU**: **yīlóu** "first floor," **èrlóu** "second floor," **jǐlóu?** "which floor?"

Months of the year with **YUÈ**: **yīyuè** "January," **èryuè** "February," **sānyuè** "March," **sìyuè** "April," **wǔyuè** "May," **liùyuè** "June," **qíyuè** "July," **báyuè** "August," **jiǔyuè** "September," **shíyuè** "October," **shíyīyuè** "November," **shí'èryuè** "December," **jǐyuè** "which month of the year?"

NIÁN as measure for "year": **yìnián** "one year," **jǐnián** "how many years?" **měinián** "every year"

SHI...-DE to express time or place of known past actions: **Wǒ shi yī-jiǔ-bā-wǔ-nián chūshēngde.** "I was born in 1985."

Time when before place: **Wǒ shi yī-jiǔ-bā-wǔ-nián zài Měiguo chūshēngde.** "I was born in 1985 in America."

Years of the calendar with **NIÁN**: **yī-jiǔ-bā-wǔ-nián** "1985"

Unit 4, Part 3: New Vocabulary and Grammar

Vocabulary

báitiān	in the daytime [TW]
cì	time [M]
dàyuē	approximately, about [A]
dì-	(forms ordinal numbers) [SP]
fángjiān	room [N]
-guo	(indicates experience) [P]
hòunián	year after next [TW]
hòutiān	day after tomorrow [TW]
huíguó	return to one's home country [VO]
huíjiā	return to one's home [VO]
jiā	family, home [PW]
jiǔ	be long (of time) [SV]
m	(hesitation sound; pause filler) [I]
qiánnián	year before last [TW]
qiántiān	day before yesterday [TW]
ránhòu	afterward, then [MA]
shuō	say, speak [V]
yào	be going to, will [AV]
yèli	at night [TW]
zhōngwǔ	noon [TW]
zhù	live (in), stay (in) [V]

Grammar

Dì- to create ordinal numbers: **dìyī** "first," **dì'èrge** "the second one," **dìsāncì** "the third time"

-GUO to express experience: **Wǒ qùguo.** "I've gone there." OR "I've been there."

Unit 4, Part 4: New Vocabulary and Grammar

Vocabulary

-băiwàn	million [NU]
Běijīng	Beijing [PW]
bǐjiào	comparatively, relatively [A]
chángcháng	often [A]
chídào	arrive late, be late [V]
duō	be many, much, more [SV]
Guăngzhōu	Guangzhou, Canton [PW]
hăoxiàng	apparently, it seems to me [MA]
kè	class [N]
Nánjīng	Nanjing [PW]
-qiānwàn	ten million [NU]
rénkŏu	population [N]
Shànghăi	Shanghai [PW]
shàngkè	have class [VO]
shăo	be few, less [SV]
shíwàn	hundred thousand [NU]
Sūn	Sun [SN]
Táiběi	Taipei [PW]
táokè	skip class [VO]
-wàn	ten thousand [NU]
Xī'ān	Xian [PW]
-yì	hundred million [NU]

Grammar

DUŌ to express "more than": **yìbăiduō rén** "more than a hundred people," **yìqiānduōkuài** "more than a thousand dollars"

HĂOXIÀNG: **Tāmen hăoxiàng hái méi lái.** "It seems they haven't come yet."

Large numbers: **yíwàn** "ten thousand," **shíwàn** "one hundred thousand," **yìbăiwàn** "one million," **yìqiānwàn** "ten million," **yíyì** "one hundred million," **shíyì** "billion"

Unit 5, Part 1: New Vocabulary and Grammar

Vocabulary

bǎ	(for chairs, umbrellas) [M]
bàngōngshì	office [PW]
bàoqiàn	feel sorry, regret [V]
búguò	however [CJ]
dāngrán	of course [MA]
Huáqiáo	overseas Chinese [N]
kéyi	may, can [AV]
lǎobǎn	boss, owner [N]
líu	leave (someone something) [V]
nàr	there [PW]
shízài	really, truly [A]
tiáozi	note [N]
xiǎng	want to, would like to [AV]
yàoshi	if [MA]
Yīngwén	English (language) [N]
yǐzi	chair [N]
zài	be present; be located at [V]
zěmme bàn	"what should be done?" [IE]
zhāng	(for tables, name cards) [M]
zhǎo	look for [V]
zhèr	here [PW]
zhīdao	know [V]
zhuōzi	table [N]

Grammar

Deletion of second syllable of bisyllabic verbs in affirmative part of affirmative-negative questions: **kéyi bu kéyi → kě bu kéyi** "may I or may I not?"

Embedded questions: **Nǐ zhīdao tā zài nǎr ma?** "Do you know where she is?"

GĚI as coverb: **Wǒ gěi tā líu yíge tiáozi** "I'm going to leave a note for her."

YÀOSHI: **Yàoshi nǐ zhǎo yíge rén.../Nǐ yàoshi zhǎo yíge rén...** "If you're looking for a person..."

ZÀI as main verb: **Tā zài bu zài?** "Is she present?," **Tā zài Niǔyuē.** "She is in New York."

-ZI as a noun suffix: **zhuōzi** "table," **yǐzi** "chair"

Unit 5, Part 2: New Vocabulary and Grammar

Vocabulary

Běidà	Peking University [PW]
cài	food [N]
cháng	often [A]
chǎng	factory [N]
chī	eat [V]
chīfàn	eat food, eat [VO]
dàxuéshēng	college student [N]
fàn	rice (cooked); food [N]
gōngrén	worker, laborer [N]
Hànyǔ	Chinese (language) [N]
kuài	soon, quickly [A]
péixùn	train [V]
pí	leather, skin [N]
píxié	leather shoe [N]
wǎnfàn	dinner, evening meal [N]
wèizi	seat, place [N]
wǔfàn	lunch [N]
xié	shoe [N]
xué	learn, study [V]
xuésheng	student [N]
zǎofàn	breakfast [N]
zhōngfàn	lunch [N]
zhōngxīn	center [N]

Grammar

College and university abbreviations: **Běijīng Dàxué → Běidà** "Beijing University"

KUÀI (YÀO)...LE to indicate an imminent action or situation: **Tā kuài yào zǒule.** "She will be leaving soon."

LÁI + Verb to indicate purpose: **Tā lái zhèr xué Zhōngwén.** "She's coming here to study Chinese."

Verb-Object compounds: **chīfàn** "eat rice" → "eat," **shuìjiào** "sleep"

ZÀI as coverb: **Wǒ zài yìjiā gōngsī gōngzuò.** "I work at a company."

Unit 5, Part 3: New Vocabulary and Grammar

Vocabulary

bān	move (a thing or one's home) [V]
běibiān(r)	north [PW]
cèsuǒ	toilet [PW]
Cháng Chéng	Great Wall [PW]
Cháng Chéng Fàndiàn	Great Wall Hotel [PW]
chéng	city [N]
-dào	arrive at, to [PV]
dìfang	place [N]
dōngbiān(r)	east [PW]
fàndiàn	hotel [PW]
huí	time [M]
kě	indeed, certainly [A]
méi shì(r)	"it's nothing," "never mind" [IE]
nánbiān(r)	south [PW]
něibiān(r)	which side, where [QW]
nèibian(r)	that side, there [PW]
pàng	be fat (of people or animals) [SV]
ràng	let, cause, make [CV]
ràng nǐ jiǔ děngle	"made you wait a long time" [IE]
shān	mountain, hill [N]
shòu	be thin, lean, skinny [SV]
Xiāng Shān	Fragrant Hills [PW]
xiāng	be fragrant, smell good [SV]
xībiān(r)	west [PW]
yāo	one [NU]
-zài	at, in, on [PV]
zhèibian(r)	this side, here [PW]

Grammar

-DÀO as postverb: **Tāmen qùnián bāndao Táiběi le.** "Last year they moved to Taipei."

Points of the compass: **dōngbiān(r)** "east, east side," **nánbiān(r)** "south, south side," **xībiān(r)** "west, west side," **běibiān(r)** "north, north side"

Stative Verb + **(YÌ)DIǍN(R)**: **piányi yìdiǎnr** "a little cheaper," **hǎo yìdiǎn** "a little better"

-ZÀI as postverb: **Wǒ zhùzai Nánjīng.** "I live in Nanjing."

Unit 5, Part 4: New Vocabulary and Grammar

Vocabulary

āiyò	(indicates surprise) [I]
diànnǎo	computer [N]
dǐxia	underneath [PW]
dōngxi	thing [N]
e	(hesitation sound; pause filler) [I]
gǒu(r)	dog [N]
guǎn	concern oneself with [V]
hòu	in back, back [L]
hòubian(r)/hòumian/hòutou	in back, back [PW]
kāiguān	switch [N]
lǐ	in, inside [L]
lǐbian(r)/lǐmiàn/lǐtou	in, inside [PW]
pángbiān(r)	at or on the side, next to [PW]
qián	in front, front [L]
qiánbian(r)/qiánmian/qiántou	in front, front [PW]
shàng	on top, on [L]
shàngbian(r)/shàngmian/shàngtou	on top, on [PW]
shǐyòng	use, employ [V]
shǐyòng shǒucè	operating manual [PH]
shǒucè	handbook, manual [N]
shūfáng	study [PW]
shūjià	bookshelf, bookcase [N]
tā	it (animal or thing) [PN]
tái	(for computers, TV sets) [M]
wài	outside [L]
wàibian(r)/wàimian/wàitou	outside [PW]
wǔ-bā-liù	Pentium® (brand of computer) [N]
xià	on the bottom, under, below [L]
xiàbian(r)/xiàmian/xiàtou	on the bottom, under, below [PW]
yào	want to [AV]
yòu	right [L]
yòubian(r)	right side, right [PW]
zuǒ	left [L]
zuǒbian(r)	left side, left [PW]

Grammar

-LE in sentences with quantified objects to indicate completed action: **Wǒ mǎile yìtái xīn diànnǎo** "I bought a new computer."

Localizers: **fángjiānli** "in the room," **zhuōzishang** "on the table"

Place Words: **lǐmiàn/lǐtou/lǐbian(r)** "inside"; **wàibian(r)/wàimian/wàitou** "outside"; **qiánbian(r)/qiánmian/qiántou** "in front"; **hòubian(r)/hòumian/hòutou** "in back"; **shàngbian(r)/shàngmian/shàngtou** "on top"; **xiàbian(r)/xiàmian/xiàtou** "on the bottom"; **zuǒbian(r)** "left side," **yòubian(r)** "right side," **pángbiān(r)** "on the side, next to"; **dǐxia** "underneath"

Unit 6, Part 1: New Vocabulary and Grammar

Vocabulary

āyí	aunt (mother's sister) [N]
chū'èr	second year in junior high school [TW]
chūsān	third year in junior high school [TW]
chūyī	first year in junior high school [TW]
chūzhōng	junior high school [PW]
dà'èr	sophomore year in college [TW]
dàsān	junior year in college [TW]
dàsì	senior year in college [TW]
dàyī	first year in college [TW]
gāo'èr	junior year in high school [TW]
gāosān	senior year in high school [TW]
gāoyī	sophomore year in high school [TW]
gāozhōng	senior high school [PW]
-gěi	give; for, to [PV]
hǎochī	be good to eat, delicious [SV]
hǎokàn	be good-looking [SV]
lǐwù	gift, present [N]
m	(indicates something tastes delicious) [I]
nánpéngyou	boyfriend, male friend [N]
niánjí	grade, level (in school) [N]
nǚpéngyou	girlfriend, female friend [N]
péngyou	friend [N]
shàng	go to, attend [V]
shūshu	uncle (father's younger brother) [N]
sòng	give (as a present) [V]
táng	candy; sugar [N]
xiǎoxué	elementary school [PW]
xǐhuan	like [AV/V]
yìniánjí	first grade [TW]
zhēn	really [A]
zhōngxué	middle school [PW]

Grammar

School system and grade in school: **xiǎoxué sānniánjí** "third grade in elementary school," **chūyī** "seventh grade," **gāo'èr** "eleventh grade," **dàsān** "junior year in college," **jǐniánjí** "which grade?"

Unit 6, Part 2: New Vocabulary and Grammar

Vocabulary

bānjiā	move one's home [VO]
-dà	big [RE]
ei	(indicates liveliness) [P]
érzi	son [N]
jiéhūn	marry, get married [VO]
jīn	gold [BF]
Jīn	gold [SN]
jiù	be old (of things) [SV]
Jiùjīnshān	San Francisco [PW]
kànqilai	in the looking [RC]
líhūn	divorce, get divorced [VO]
nàli	there [PW]
náli	where [QW]
niánqīng	be young [SV]
Niǔyuē	New York [PW]
nǚ'ér	daughter [N]
-qǐlai	in the VERBing [RE]
xiǎohái(r)	small child, kid [N]
yìsi	meaning [N]
zhǎng	grow [V]
zhǎngdà	grow up [RC]
zhèli	here [PW]
zuò	do, make [V]

Grammar

-QILAI to indicate "in the VERBing": **Tā kànqilai hěn lǎo.** "She looks very old."

Unit 6, Part 3: New Vocabulary and Grammar

Vocabulary

dōngběi	northeast [PW]
dōngnán	southeast [PW]
fúwù	serve [V]
hángkōng	aviation [N]
hángkōng gōngsī	airline [PH]
jiāo	teach [V]
jiāoshū	teach [VO]
Měiguo Zài Tái Xiéhuì	American Institute in Taiwan [PW]
méiyou	(indicates past negative of action verbs) [AV]
néng	be able to, can [AV]
shàngbān(r)	work, go to work [VO]
shàngxué	attend school [VO]
suóyi	therefore, so [CJ]
Táiběi Měiguo Xuéxiào	Taipei American School [PW]
wèishemme	why [QW]
xiàbān(r)	get off from work [VO]
xīběi	northwest [PW]
xiéhuì	association, society [N]
xī'nán	southwest [PW]
Xī'nán Hángkōng Gōngsī	Southwest Airlines® [PW]
xuéxiào	school [PW]
yīnwei	because [MA]

Grammar

Intermediate points of the compass: **dōngnán** "southeast," **dōngběi** "northeast," **xī'nán** "southwest," **xīběi** "northwest"

JIĀO and **JIĀOSHŪ**: **Wǒ xǐhuan jiāoshū.** "I like to teach." **Shéi jiāo nǐmen Yīngwén?** "Who is teaching you English?"

MÉIYOU to indicate past negative of action verbs: **Tā méiyou qù.** "She didn't go."

YĪNWEI...SUÓYI...: **Tā yīnwei hěn máng, suóyi bù néng lái.** "Because she's busy, she can't come."

Unit 6, Part 4: New Vocabulary and Grammar

Vocabulary

Àodàliyà	Australia [PW]
Àozhōu	Australia [PW]
dàmèi	older younger sister
fùmǔ	parents [N]
gěi	give [V]
gēn	with [CV]
Huáng	Huang (lit. "yellow") [SN]
jiěmèi	older and younger sisters [N]
jīhui	opportunity, chance [N]
lǎo-	(indicates rank among siblings) [BF]
lǎodà	oldest (among siblings) [N]
liáo	chat [V]
liáotiān	chat [VO]
liúxué	study as a foreign student [VO]
páiháng	one's seniority among siblings [N]
wàizǔfù	maternal grandfather [N]
wàizǔmǔ	maternal grandmother [N]
wàng	forget [V]
xiǎomèi	younger younger sister [N]
xiōngdì	older and younger brothers [N]
yǐhòu	in the future [TW]
yímín	immigrate, emigrate [V]
Zhèng	Zheng [SN]
zìwǒ jièshao	introduce oneself [PH]
zǔfù	paternal grandfather [N]
zǔmǔ	paternal grandmother [N]

Grammar

...-LE...LE in sentences with non-quantified objects to indicate completed action: **Wǒ wàngle zìwǒ jièshaole.** "I forgot to introduce myself."

Unit 7, Part 1: New Vocabulary and Grammar

Vocabulary

biǎojiě	older female cousin of different surname [N]
biǎojiěfu	husband of older female cousin of different surname [N]
cóngqián	in the past, formerly [TW]
gǎiháng	change one's line of work [VO]
gōngchǎng	factory [PW]
hái	in addition [A]
hé	and [CJ]
kǒu	(for people; lit. "mouth") [M]
mǎimài	business [N]
nánháir	boy [N]
ne	(pause filler) [P]
nǚháir	girl [N]
shēnti	body [N]
xiàn	county [N]
yòu'éryuán	kindergarten [PW]
yuánlái	originally, formerly [MA]
zuò mǎimài	do or engage in business [PH]

Grammar

Choice-type questions with choice implied: **Nánháir nǚháir?** "A boy or a girl?" **Nǐ yào zhèige yào nèige?** "Do you want this one or do you want that one?"

. . . .

Unit 7, Part 2: New Vocabulary and Grammar

Vocabulary

Běijīng Yǔyán Wénhuà Dàxué	Beijing Language and Culture University [PW]
bú cuò	"not bad," "quite good" [IE]
Déyǔ	German (language) [N]
-de	(verb suffix that indicates manner) [P]
Fǎyǔ	French (language) [N]
Hànzì	Chinese character [N]
huà	word, language [N]
huì	know how to, can [AV]
jǐ-	a few, several [NU]
jìxù	continue [V]
ma	(indicates something obvious) [P]
Pǔtōnghuà	Mandarin (language) [N]
qítā	other [AT]
quán	completely [A]
rènshi	recognize [V]
Rìyǔ	Japanese (language) [N]
shuōhuà	speak words, speak [VO]
Xībānyáyǔ	Spanish (language) [N]
xiě	write [V]
xiězì(r)	write characters, write [VO]
ya	(form of particle **a** used after words ending in **-a** or **-i**) [P]
Yīngyǔ	English (language) [N]
yǐqián	before, formerly [TW]
yǒude	some [AT]
Zhōngguo huà	spoken Chinese [PH]
Zhōngguo zì(r)	Chinese character [PH]

Grammar

Equivalents of "can": **huì** "know how," **néng** "be physically able," **kéyi** "have permission to"

Equivalents of "know": **huì** "know how," **zhīdao** "know a fact," **rènshi** "be acquainted with"

-DE after verbs to indicate manner: **Tā Zhōngguo huà shuōde hěn hǎo.** "She speaks Chinese very well." **Tā xiě Zhōngguo zì xiěde hěn hǎokàn.** "He writes Chinese characters very attractively."

MA to indicate an obvious situation: **Nínde Hànyǔ shuōde tǐng bú cuò ma!** "You speak Chinese quite well, you know!"

Names of languages

Question words used as indefinites: **Wǒ rènshi jǐbǎige Zhōngguo zì.** "I know a few hundred Chinese characters." **Wǒ zhǐ yǒu jǐkuài qián.** "I only have a few dollars."

Terms for "Chinese language"

YǑUDE...YǑUDE...: **Yǒude láile, yǒude méi lái.** "Some came, some didn't come." **Yǒude wǒ mǎile, yǒude méi mǎi.** "I bought some, I didn't buy others."

Unit 7, Part 3: New Vocabulary and Grammar

Vocabulary

duàn(r)	section, segment, period (of time) [M]
hé	with [CV]
hòulái	afterward, later [TW]
jiǎng	speak, say [V]
jiǎnghuà	speak, talk [VO]
kāishǐ	begin [V]; in the beginning [TW]
nánguài...	no wonder... [PT]
nèmme	like that, so [A]
shíhou(r)	time [N]
yíge rén	by oneself, alone [PH]
yìqǐ	together [A]
yòu	again [A]
yǒude shíhou(r)	sometimes [PH]
yuǎn	be far away [SV]
yuèfen(r)	month [N]

Grammar

HÉ...YÌQǏ and GĒN...YÌQǏ: Wǒmen hé tāmen yìqǐ qù ba! "Let's go together with them!"

NÁNGUÀI...: Nánguài nǐde Hànyǔ jiǎngde zhèmme hǎo. "No wonder that you speak Chinese so well."

SHI...-DE to express attendant circumstances of known past actions: **Wǒ shi hé wǒ àirén yìqǐ láide.** "I came together with my spouse."

Unit 7, Part 4: New Vocabulary and Grammar

Vocabulary

bàng	be great, wonderful [SV]
bìyè	graduate [PT]
chà	be lacking, deficient [SV]
cóng	from [CV]
duōshù	the majority [N]
fùyu	be prosperous [SV]
gǔ	be ancient [SV]
jiù	only [A]
juéde	feel [V]
nèiyang(r)	that way, like that [MA]
niàn	study [V]
nǔlì	be diligent, work hard [SV]
shēnqǐng	apply [V]
tīngshuō	hear of, hear it said that [V]
yánjiū	research [V/N]
yánjiūshēng	graduate student [N]
...yǐhòu	after... [PT]
...yǐqián	before..., ...ago [PT]
zhèiyang(r)	this way, like this [MA]
...zhīhòu	after... [PT]
...zhīqián	before..., ...ago [PT]
zhì'ān	public order, public security [N]

Grammar

Backchannel comments: **Ò.** "Oh," **Zhèiyang.** "So this is how it is."

BÌYÈ: Tā shi Běidà bìyède. "She graduated from Beijing University."

Phrase + **YǏQIÁN/ZHĪQIÁN** and Phrase + **YǏHÒU/ZHĪHÒU: Tā shi yìnián yǐqián qù Zhōngguode.** "He went to China one year ago." **Tā liǎngge yuè zhīhòu yào jiéhūn.** "She's going to get married in two months."

Unit 8, Part 1: New Vocabulary and Grammar

Vocabulary

běi	north [L]
běifāng	north, the North [PW]
běifāng huà	northern speech [PH]
běifāng rén	Northerner [PH]
Běijīng Fàndiàn	Beijing Hotel [PW]
dǎdī	take a taxi [VO]
dàgài	probably, about [MA]
dōngfāng	east, the East [PW]
Dōngfāng rén	Asian person [PH]
gèng	even more, more [A]
guò	pass, go by [V]
huòzhě	or [CJ]
jìn	be close, near [SV]
kāi	drive, operate a vehicle [V]
kuài	be fast [SV]
láojià	excuse me [IE]
lí	be distant from, from [CV]
nán	south [L]
nánfāng	south, the South [PW]
nánfāng huà	southern speech [PH]
nánfāng rén	Southerner [PH]
Tiān'ānmén	Tiananmen [PW]
wàng	to, toward [CV]
xī	west [L]
xīfāng	west, the West [PW]
Xīfāng rén	Westerner [PH]
yìzhí	straight [A]
zǒu	go, walk [V]
zǒulù	walk [VO]
zuǒyòu	about, approximately [PW]

Grammar

Conditional clauses with **-DE HUÀ**: **Zǒulùde huà, dàgài yào bàn'ge zhōngtóu zuǒyòu.** "If you walk, it will probably take about half an hour."

LÍ to express distance from: **Nǐ jiā lí zhèr yuǎn bu yuǎn?** "Is your home far from here?" **Wǒ jiā lí zhèr hěn jìn.** "My home is close to here."

QÙ...ZĚMME ZǑU: **Láojià, qù Wàijiāobù zěmme zǒu?** "Excuse me, how do you get to the Foreign Ministry?"

WÀNG to express movement toward a certain direction: **wàng xī zǒu** "walk toward the west," **wàng qián kāi** "drive forward"

ZUǑYÒU: **liǎngge yuè zuǒyòu** "about two months"

Unit 8, Part 2: New Vocabulary and Grammar

Vocabulary

Běijīng Wàiguoyǔ Dàxué	Beijing Foreign Studies University [PW]
Běiwài	(abbreviation for Beijing Foreign Studies University) [PW]
bīnguǎn	guest house, hotel [PW]
chēzi	car, vehicle [N]
chūzū	rent out [V]
chūzū qìchē	taxi [PH]
Fù	Fu [SN]
hǎode	"all right," "O.K." [IE]
jīchǎng	airport [PW]
liàng	(for land vehicles) [M]
lóu	building (with two or more floors) [N]
ménkǒu(r)	doorway, entrance [PW]
qìchē	car, vehicle [N]
shǒudū	capital [N]
Shǒudū Jīchǎng	Capital Airport [PW]
wàiguo	foreign country [N]
wàiguo huà	foreign language [PH]
wàiguo rén	foreigner [PH]
wàiguoyǔ	foreign language [N]
wéi	"hello" [I]
xìngmíng	first and last name [N]
Yǒuyì Bīnguǎn	Friendship Hotel [PW]
yǒuyì	friendship [N]
zhuānjiā	expert [N]
zhuānjiā lóu	(foreign) experts' building [PH]

Grammar

Pivot sentences: **Wǒ yào yíliàng chē qù Shǒudū Jīchǎng** "I want a car to go to Capital Airport"

Unit 8, Part 3: New Vocabulary and Grammar

Vocabulary

dǎ	hit [V]
dǎ diànhuà	make a telephone call [PH]
diànhuà	telephone [N]
fázi	means, method, way [N]
gǎn	rush, hurry [V]
huì	be likely to, will [AV]
jiāotōng	traffic [N]
jìnkuài	as fast as possible [A]
juédìng	decide [V]
máfan	trouble, disturb [V]
mǎshàng	immediately, right away [A]
nàixīn	be patient/patience [SV/N]
pài	dispatch, send [V]
pàiqu	dispatch, send out [RC]
-qu	(indicates motion away from the speaker) [RE]
shàng	go to, come to, to [CV]
sījī	driver, chauffeur [N]
tōngzhī	notify [V]
xiǎoshí	hour [N]
yào	need to, have to, should [AV]; request [V]
yìhuǐr	a while [N]
yōngjǐ	be crowded [SV]
zěmme	how come, why [QW]
zháojí	worry, get excited [SV/VO]

Grammar

Resultative compounds: **pàiqu** "send out," **láibují** "not be able to make it on time"

. . . .

Unit 8, Part 4: New Vocabulary and Grammar

Vocabulary

bàntiān	"half the day," a long time [NU+M]
biéde	other, another [AT]
dǔchē	be clogged up with cars [VO]
gōngjīn	kilo [M]
huàn	change to, exchange [V]
jiàn	(for luggage, matters) [M]
kāichē	drive a car [VO]
mǐ	meter [M]
qīng	be light (not heavy) [SV]
sāichē	be clogged up with cars [VO]
shīfu	master; driver [N]
tiáo	(for streets, alleys) [M]
xíngli	luggage, baggage [N]
xūyào	need [V]
yīngdāng	should, ought to [AV]
zāogāo	be a mess [SV]; "darn it," "what a mess" [IE]
zhǎo	give in change [V]
zhǎoqián	give (someone) change [VO]
zhǐhǎo	have no choice but [A]
zhòng	be heavy [SV]
zuìhòu	in the end, finally [TW]

Grammar

CÓNG...DÀO...: **Cóng sāndiǎn bàn dào wǔdiǎn.** "From 3:30 until 5:00."

Height and weight: **Nǐ duō zhòng?** "How heavy are you?" **Wǒ liùshisāngōngjīn.** "I weigh 63 kilos." **Nǐ duō gāo?** "How tall are you?" **Wǒ yīmǐ bā'èr.** "I'm one meter eighty-two."

Specifier + Number + Measure + Noun: **zhèiliǎngjiàn xíngli** "these two pieces of luggage"

ZHǏHǍO: **Wǒmen zhǐhǎo huí sùshè.** "We have no choice but to return to our dorm."

Unit 9, Part 1: New Vocabulary and Grammar

Vocabulary

bái	be white [SV]
báisè	the color white [N]
běndì	this place, here [N]
bú yòng	not need to, don't need to [AV]
bú yòng xiè	"don't mention it" [IE]
dēng	light, lamp [N]
guǎi	turn [V]
hēi	be black [SV]
hēisè	the color black [N]
Hépíng Bīnguǎn	Peace Hotel [PW]
hóng	be red [SV]
hónglǜdēng	traffic light [N]
hóngsè	the color red [N]
huáng	be yellow [SV]
huángsè	the color yellow [N]
jiāotōng jǐngchá	traffic police [PH]
jiāotōngjǐng	traffic police [N]
jǐngchá	police [N]
lán	be blue [SV]
lánsè	the color blue [N]
lǜ	be green [SV]
lùkǒu(r)	intersection [PW]
lǜsè	the color green [N]
qīngchu	be clear, clear about [SV]
xiè	thank [V]
yánsè	color [N]
zhuǎn	turn [V]

Grammar

Chinese equivalents of English "ask": **Nǐ yàoshi bù dǒngde huà, yào wèn lǎoshī a!** "If you don't under-stand, you should ask the teacher!" **Qǐng tā míngtiān zài lái.** "Ask him to come again tomorrow." **Lǎoshī jiào wǒmen zuò zuòyè.** "The teacher asked us to do our homework."

Color terms

Unit 9, Part 2: New Vocabulary and Grammar

Vocabulary

búbì	don't need to, not be necessary [AV]
chēzhàn	bus stop; bus station [PW]
diànchē	street car, trolley, tram [N]
dòngwù	animal [N]
dòngwùyuán(r)	zoo [PW]
gōnggòng	public [AT]
gōnggòng qìchē	public bus, bus [PH]
lù	(for bus routes) [M]
māo(r)	cat [N]
niǎo(r)	bird [N]
shàngchē	get on a vehicle [VO]
yǎng	raise, keep [V]
Yíhéyuán	Summer Palace [PW]
yú(r)	fish [N]
zhàn	station, stop [N]
zhī	(for most animals) [M]
zhōngdiǎn	final or terminal point [N]
zhōngdiǎn zhàn	last station, last stop [PH]

Grammar

XIĀN...RÁNHÒU... "First...then...": **Xiān chīfàn ránhòu zài qù mǎi dōngxi.** "First eat and then go shopping."

Unit 9, Part 3: New Vocabulary and Grammar

Vocabulary

bèn	be stupid [SV]
búdàn	not only [A]
cōngming	be smart [SV]
érqiě	moreover, and, also [CJ]
gāng	just now, just [A]
gānggāng	just now, just [A]
gānjìng	be clean [SV]
jiào	call (someone) [V]
kāi wánxiào	joke around, play a prank [PH]
lǎn	be lazy [SV]
luàn	be disorderly, messy [SV]
méi	not have [V]
piào	ticket [N]
shàng	get on [V]
shēngqì	get angry [SV/VO]
shòupiàoyuán	ticketseller, conductor [N]
shuō xiàohua(r)	tell a joke [PH]
wánxiào	joke [N]
xīwàng	hope [V]
yònggōng	be hardworking, studious [SV]
zāng	be dirty [SV]
zhěngqí	be in order, neat [SV]

Grammar

BÚDÀN...ÉRQIĚ... "Not only...but also...": **Tā búdàn niánqīng, érqiě cōngmíng.** "She's not only young, but also smart."

Unit 9, Part 4: New Vocabulary and Grammar

Vocabulary

chēpiào	bus ticket [N]
chūshì	show, produce [V]
-dào	(indicates action of verb is realized) [RE]
dǒng	understand [V]
-dǒng	understand [RE]
gāi	should [AV]
jìde	remember [V]
kàn	read [V]
kàndǒng	read and understand [RC]
ne	(indicates continuous aspect) [P]
shuìzháo	fall asleep [RC]
tīng	hear, listen [V]
tīngdǒng	hear and understand [RC]
tóngzhì	comrade [N]
wèi	"hey" [I]
xiàchē	get off a vehicle [VO]
xiǎoxīn	be careful [SV]
yuèpiào	monthly ticket [N]
zǎo	be early [SV]
-zháo	(indicates action of verb is realized) [RE]
zhǎodào	look for and find, find [RC]
zhǎozháo	look for and find, find [RC]
-zhe	(indicates continuous aspect) [P]
zhǔnbèi	prepare, get ready, plan [V]

Grammar

Potential resultative compounds: **zhǎo** "look for," **zhǎozháo** "look for and find," **zhǎodezháo** "be able to find," **zhǎobuzháo** "be unable to find"

-ZHE as continuous aspect suffix: **zǎozhe ne** "it's (continuing being) early"

Unit 10, Part 1: New Vocabulary and Grammar

Vocabulary

āiyà	"oh," "gosh" [I]
biàn	change [V]
-chéng	become; into [PV]
dǎléi	thunder [VO]
dī	be low [SV]
dù	degree (of temperature) [M]
éi	(introduces questions) [I]
...éryǐ	only [PT]
kěnéng	be possible [AV]
qíngtiān	fine day, sunny day [N]
rè	be hot [SV]
shǎndiàn	lightning strikes [VO]
suóyi shuō	so, therefore [PH]
tiān	sky [N]
tiānqi	weather [N]
tiānqi yùbào	weather forecast [PH]
wēndù	temperature [N]
xiàyǔ	rain [VO]
yídìng	definitely [A]
yīntiān	cloudy or overcast weather [N]
yǔ	rain [N]
yùbào	forecast [N]
yuè lái yuè...	more and more... [PT]
yún	cloud [N]
zǎo	"good morning" [IE]
zhǔn	be accurate [SV]
zuì	most [A]

Grammar

CÓNG...KĀISHǏ: **cóng míngtiān kāishǐ** "starting from tomorrow"

DÙ to express temperatures: **shíbādù** "eighteen degrees"

...ÉRYǏ "and that's all": **Wǒ zhǐ yǒu yìbǎikuài éryǐ.** "I only have one hundred dollars and that's all."

YUÈ LÁI YUÈ... "more and more": **Tiānqi yuè lái yuè rè.** "The weather has been getting hotter and hotter."

Unit 10, Part 2: New Vocabulary and Grammar

Vocabulary

chū tàiyáng	the sun comes/is out [PH]
chūntiān	spring [TW]
dōngtiān	winter [TW]
fēng	wind [N]
fēngshā	wind and sand; blowing sand [N]
gān	be dry [SV]
hěn shǎo	seldom [PH]
héshì	be appropriate [SV]
jìjié	season [N]
lěng	be cold [SV]
qiūtiān	fall, autumn [TW]
rúguǒ	if [MA]
shā	sand, gravel [N]
shūfu	be comfortable [SV]
sǐ	die [V]
tàiyáng	sun [N]
wán(r)	play, have a good time [V]
xiàtiān	summer [TW]
xiàxuě	snow [VO]
xuě	snow [N]
yào	if [MA]
zhèmme shuō	saying it like this; then [PH]
zhèng	just [A]

Grammar

BÙ...YĚ BÙ... "neither...nor...": **Tā shuō Zhōngwén bù nán yě bù róngyi.** "She said that Chinese was neither hard nor easy."

RÚGUǑ...JIÙ... "if...then...": **Rúguǒ xiàyǔde huà, wǒmen jiù bú qù.** "If it should rain, we (then) won't go."

YÒU...YÒU... "both...and...": **Nèige xuésheng yòu cōngmíng yòu yònggōng.** "That student is both smart and diligent."

Unit 10, Part 3: New Vocabulary and Grammar

Vocabulary

bànfǎ(r)	way of doing something, method [N]
cháoshī	be humid [SV]
chūlái	come out [RC]
-chūlái	come out [RE]
chūmén(r)	go outside [VO]
chūqu	go out [RC]
dànshi	but [CJ]
gēnběn (+ NEGATIVE)	(not) at all [A]
jìnlái	come in [RC]
-jìnlái	come in [RE]
jìnqu	go in [RC]
kànchūlái	know something by looking [RC]
kōngqì	air [N]
m	(indicates agreement) [I]
máomáoyǔ	light rain [N]
nèiyangzi	that way, like that [MA]
pèng	bump, run into [V]
pèngshang	run into, meet with, encounter [RC]
piāo	float [V]
piāojìnlái	float in [RC]
qíshí	actually [MA]
shāchuāng	screen window [N]
-shàng	up, on [RE]
táifēng	typhoon [N]
wù	fog [N]
xià máomáoyǔ	drizzle [PH]
Yángmíng Shān	Yangming Mountain [PW]
yùnqi	luck [N]
zài	(indicates progressive aspect) [AV]
zhèiyangzi	this way, like this [MA]

Grammar

Directional Verbs: **jìnlái** "come in," **jìnqu** "go in," **chūlái** "come out," **chūqu** "go out," **piāojìnlái** "float in," **kànbuchūlái** "be unable to know something by looking"

HǍOXIÀNG...-DE YÀNGZI "seem like...": **Hǎoxiàng wù cóng shāchuāng piāojìnláide yàngzi.** "It seems as though the fog is floating in through the window screen."

Noun suffix **-FǍ** "way of doing something": **bànfǎ** "way of doing something," **kànfǎ** "way of looking at things," **xiǎngfǎ** "way of thinking," **xiěfǎ** "way of writing," etc.

Reduplication of measures and nouns to indicate "every": **tiān** "day" → **tiāntiān** "every day," **nián** "year" → **niánnián** "every year," **rén** "person" → **rénrén** "everybody"

ZÀI as auxiliary verb to indicate progressive aspect: **Tā zài chīfàn.** "He's eating."

Unit 10, Part 4: New Vocabulary and Grammar

Vocabulary

Àomén	Macao [PW] (10-4)
bǐ	compare [CV/V]
chàbuduō	not lack much, be good enough [IE]
...-de shíhou(r)	when... [PT]
dōngàn	east coast [PW]
dōng-nuǎn-xià-liáng	"warm in winter, cool in summer" [EX]
fēngjǐng	scenery [N]
gānzào	be dry [SV]
Jiāzhōu	California [PW]
liángkuai	be comfortably cool [SV]
měi	be beautiful [SV]
Měijí Huárén	Chinese with U.S. nationality [PH]
nánguò	be sad [SV]
nuǎnhuo	be warm [SV]
qìhou	climate [N]
shìyìng	adapt, get used to [V]
wǎn	be late [SV]
xī'àn	west coast [PW]
xíguàn	be accustomed to [V]

Grammar

BǏ to express unequal comparison: **Tā bǐ wǒ gāo.** "He is taller than me."

...DE SHÍHOU(R) "when": **Tā gàosu wǒde shíhou, yǐjīng tài wǎnle.** "When he told me, it was already too late."

A **MÉIYOU** B **NÈMME/ZHÈMME** C "A is not as C as B": **Wǒ méiyou tā nèmme gāo.** "I'm not as tall as him."

2. Substitution Drills

Unit 1, Part 1: Substitution Drills

Listen to the audio; after each prompt, say the new sentence using that substitution. Do each drill at least twice: first with the book open, then with the book closed. Each drill starts with a model sentence for you to repeat.

1.	**Kē Léi'ēn**	, nǐ hǎo!	Ke Leien, how are you?
	Wáng Jīngshēng		Wang Jingsheng, how are you?
	Kē Léi'ēn		Ke Leien, how are you?

2.	**Nǐ**	dào nǎr qù a?	Where are you going?
	Kē Léi'ēn		Where is Ke Leien going?
	Wáng Jīngshēng		Where is Wang Jingsheng going?
	Nǐ		Where are you going?

3.	Wǒ qù	**túshūguǎn.**	I'm going to the library.
		shítáng.	I'm going to the dining hall.
		sùshè.	I'm going to the dormitory.
		túshūguǎn.	I'm going to the library.

4.	Wǒ dào	**túshūguǎn** qù.	I'm going to the library.
		shítáng	I'm going to the cafeteria.
		sùshè	I'm going to the dormitory.
		túshūguǎn	I'm going to the library.

5.	Wǒ qù túshūguǎn.	**Nǐ** ne?	I'm going to the library. How about you?
		Kē Léi'ēn	I'm going to the library. How about Ke Leien?
		Wáng Jīngshēng	I'm going to the library. How about Wang Jingsheng?
		Nǐ	I'm going to the library. How about you?

6.	Wǒ huí	**sùshè.**	I'm going back to the dormitory.
		túshūguǎn.	I'm going back to the library.
		shítáng.	I'm going back to the cafeteria.
		sùshè.	I'm going back to the dormitory.

7.	**Wǒ**	qù bàn yìdiǎnr shìr.	I'm going to take care of a little matter.
	Kē Léi'ēn		Ke Leien is going to take care of a little matter.
	Wáng Jīngshēng		Wang Jingsheng is going to take care of a little matter.
	Wǒ		I'm going to take care of a little matter.

8.	Wǒ qù,	**Wáng Jīngshēng yě qù.**	I'm going and Wang Jingsheng is going, too.
		Kē Léi'ēn yě qù.	I'm going and Ke Leien is going, too.
		nǐ yě qù.	I'm going and you're going, too.
		Wáng Jīngshēng yě qù.	I'm going and Wang Jingsheng is going, too.

Unit 1, Part 2: Substitution Drills

Listen to the audio; after each prompt, say the new sentence using that substitution. Do each drill at least twice: first with the book open, then with the book closed. Each drill starts with a model sentence for you to repeat.

1. **Zhào Guócái**   , hǎo jiǔ bú jiànle!   Zhao Guocai, long time no see!

   Wáng Jīngshēng   Wang Jingsheng, long time no see!

   Kē Léi'ēn   Ke Leien, long time no see!

   Bàba   Dad, long time no see!

   Māma   Mom, long time no see!

   Háizi   Child, long time no see!

   Zhào Guócái   Zhao Guocai, long time no see!

2. **Nǐ**   zěmmeyàng a?   How are you?

   Tā   How is he?

   Tāmen   How are they?

   Nǐ àirén   How is your spouse?

   Wáng Jīngshēng   How is Wang Jingsheng?

   Shítáng   How is the cafeteria?

   Nǐ   How are you?

3. **Wǒ**   hái xíng.   I'm all right.

   Nǐ   You're all right.

   Tā   He's all right.

   Tāmen   They're all right.

   Wǒ bàba   My dad is all right.

   Wǒ māma   My mom is all right.

   Wǒ àirén   My spouse is all right.

   Wǒ   I'm all right.

4. **Nǐ àirén**   hǎo ma?   Is your spouse well?

   Nǐ māma   Is your mom well?

   Nǐ   Are you well?

   Tā   Is she well?

   Tāmen   Are they well?

   Zhào Guócái   Is Zhao Guocai well?

   Sùshè   Is the dormitory good?

   Nǐ àirén   Is your spouse well?

5. **Nǐ àirén, háizi**   dōu hǎo ma?   Are your spouse and children all O.K.?

   Nǐ bàba, māma   Are your mom and dad both O.K.?

   Kē Léi'ēn, Wáng Jīngshēng   Are Ke Leien and Wang Jingsheng both O.K.?

   Zhào Guócái, Wáng Jīngshēng   Are Zhao Guocai and Wang Jingsheng both O.K.?

   Tāmen   Are they all O.K.?

   Háizi   Are the children all O.K.?

   Nǐ àirén, háizi   Are your spouse and children all O.K.?

6.	**Nǐ**	bàba qù ma?	Is your father going?
	Tā		Is her father going?
	Wǒ		Is my father going?
	Nǐ		Is your father going?

7.	Tāmen dōu hěn	**hǎo.**	They are all very well.
		máng.	They are all very busy.
		lèi.	They are all very tired.
		hǎo.	They are all very well.

8.	Tāmen yě dōu	**hěn hǎo.**	They also are all very well.
		hěn máng.	They also are all very busy.
		qù.	They also are all going.
		huí sùshè.	They also are all going back to the dormitory.
		hái xíng.	They also are all alright.
		yǒu yìdiǎnr shì.	They also all have something to do.
		qù bàn yìdiǎnr shì.	They also are all going to take care of something.
		hěn hǎo.	They also are all very well.

9.	**Wǒ**	yǒu yìdiǎnr shì.	I have something to do.
	Tā		He has something to do.
	Tāmen		They have something to do.
	Zhào Guócái		Zhao Guocai has something to do.
	Wǒ bàba		My father has something to do.
	Wǒ		I have something to do.

. . . .

Unit 1, Part 3: Substitution Drills

Listen to the audio; after each prompt, say the new sentence using that substitution. Do each drill at least twice: first with the book open, then with the book closed. Each drill starts with a model sentence for you to repeat.

1. **Èi, Lǎo**	**Hé**	, nǐ hǎo a!	Hey, Old He, how are you?
	Kē		Hey, Old Ke, how are you?
	Wáng		Hey, Old Wang, how are you?
	Gāo		Hey, Old Gao, how are you?
	Zhào		Hey, Old Zhao, how are you?
	Hé		Hey, Old He, how are you?

2. Xiǎo	**Gāo**	, zuìjìn zěmmeyàng a?	Little Gao, how have you been recently?
	Hé		Little He, how have you been recently?
	Kē		Little Ke, how have you been recently?
	Wáng		Little Wang, how have you been recently?
	Zhào		Little Zhao, how have you been recently?
	Gāo		Little Gao, how have you been recently?

3. Wǒ bù	**máng.**		I'm not busy.
	jǐnzhāng.		I'm not nervous.
	lǎo.		I'm not old.
	ǎi.		I'm not short.
	zǒu.		I'm not leaving.
	máng.		I'm not busy.

4. Tā yě bú	**kùn.**		He is also not sleepy.
	lèi.		He is also not tired.
	zuò.		He is also not sitting.
	jìn.		He is also not entering.
	qù.		He is also not going.
	kùn.		He is also not sleepy.

5. Bú tài	**máng.**		Not very busy.
	lèi.		Not very tired.
	kùn.		Not very sleepy.
	gāo.		Not very tall.
	lǎo.		Not very old.
	nán.		Not very difficult.
	máng.		Not very busy.

6. Nǐ gōngzuò	máng bu máng?		Is your work busy or not?
	lèi bu lèi?		Is your work tiring or not?
	nán bu nán?		Is your work difficult or not?
	jǐnzhāng bu jǐnzhāng?		Is your work intense or not?
	róngyi bu róngyi?		Is your work easy or not?
	máng bu máng?		Is your work busy or not?

7. Tāmen zuìjìn tǐng	jǐnzhāng	de.	They have been quite nervous recently.
	lèi		They have been quite tired recently.
	kùn		They have been quite sleepy recently.
	máng		They have been quite busy recently.
	hǎo		They have been quite well recently.
	jǐnzhāng		They have been quite nervous recently.

• •

Unit 1, Part 4: Substitution Drills

Listen to the audio; after each prompt, say the new sentence using that substitution. Do each drill at least twice: first with the book open, then with the book closed. Each drill starts with a model sentence for you to repeat.

---

1. **Lín Tàitai**   , xièxie nín le!   Thank you, Mrs. Lin!

    Wáng Xiānsheng   Thank you, Mr. Wang!

    Zhào Xiáojie   Thank you, Miss Zhao!

    Xiè Tàitai   Thank you, Mrs. Xie!

    Hé Xiānsheng   Thank you, Mr. He!

    Lín Tàitai   Thank you, Mrs. Lin!

---

2. Wáng Xiānsheng, qǐng   **jìn!**   Mr. Wang, please enter!

    màn zǒu!   Mr. Wang, please take care!

    zuò!   Mr. Wang, please sit down!

    qù shítáng!   Mr. Wang, please go to the cafeteria!

    huí sùshè!   Mr. Wang, please return to the dormitory!

    jìn!   Mr. Wang, please enter!

---

3. Xiǎo Zhào, qǐng nǐ   **dào shítáng qù.**   Little Zhao, please go to the cafeteria.

    dào túshūguǎn qù.   Little Zhao, please go to the library.

    huí sùshè.   Little Zhao, please return to the dormitory.

    qù bàn yìdiǎnr shì.   Little Zhao, please go and take care of something.

    xièxie tāmen.   Little Zhao, please thank them.

    qù.   Little Zhao, please go.

    zǒu.   Little Zhao, please leave.

    dào shítáng qù.   Little Zhao, please go to the cafeteria.

---

4. Wǒ   **zǒu**   le.   I'll be going now.

    yǒu   I have it now.

    kùn   I've gotten sleepy.

    lèi   I've gotten tired.

    lǎo   I've gotten old.

    hǎo   I'm O.K. now.

    kéyi   I'm O.K. now.

    zǒu   I'll be going now.

---

5. Wǒ   **bú qù**   le.   I'm no longer going.

    bú zuò   I won't sit any longer.

    bú bàn   I don't handle it any more.

    bù zǒu   I'm not leaving anymore.

    bù xíng   I'm in a bad way now.

    bú kùn   I'm no longer tired.

    bù jǐnzhāng   I'm no longer nervous.

    bú qù   I'm no longer going.

6. Nǐ	lèi	le ma?	Have you gotten tired?
	kùn		Have you gotten sleepy?
	hǎo		Are you O.K. now?
	bú qù		Are you no longer going?
	bú bàn		Are you no longer doing it?
	lèi		Have you gotten tired?

7. Zhōngwén	yǒu yìsi	ma?	Is Chinese interesting?
	méi yìsi		Is Chinese not interesting?
	nán		Is Chinese difficult?
	róngyi		Is Chinese easy?
	yǒu yìsi		Is Chinese interesting?

8. Tāmen	gāo ma?	Are they tall?
Wǒ		Am I tall?
Nǐ		Are you tall?
Nín		Are you tall?
Tā		Is he tall?
Wǒmen		Are we tall?
Nǐmen		Are you tall?
Tāmen		Are they tall?

Unit 2, Part 1: Substitution Drills

Listen to the audio; after each prompt, say the new sentence using that substitution. Do each drill at least twice: first with the book open, then with the book closed. Each drill starts with a model sentence for you to repeat.

1. **Nǐ**   shi něiguó rén?   What country are you from?

   Nín   What country are you from?

   Tā   What country is she from?

   Xiǎo Hé   What country is Little He from?

   Lǎo Zhào   What country is Old Zhao from?

   Bái Xiáojie   What country is Miss Bai from?

   Xiè Tàitai   What country is Mrs. Xie from?

   Nǐ   What country are you from?

2. **Tā shi**   **Zhōngguo rén.**   She is Chinese.

                            Jiā'nádà rén.   She is Canadian.

                            hǎo háizi.   She is a good child.

                            Zhōngwén lǎoshī.   She is a Chinese teacher.

                            wǒ bàba.   She is my father.

                            wǒ àirén.   She is my spouse.

                            hǎo rén.   She is a good person.

                            Zhōngguo rén.   She is Chinese.

3. **Nǐ shì bu shi**   **Zhōngguo rén?**   Are you Chinese?

                            zǒngjīnglǐ?   Are you the general manager?

                            Jiā'nádà rén?   Are you Canadian?

                            Měiguo rén?   Are you American?

                            Rìběn rén?   Are you Japanese?

                            jīnglǐ?   Are you the manager?

                            Zhōngguo rén?   Are you Chinese?

4. **Wǒ bú shi**   **Zhōngguo rén.**   I'm not Chinese.

                            Táiwān rén.   I'm not Taiwanese.

                            Xībānyá rén.   I'm not Spanish.

                            Yīngguo rén.   I'm not English.

                            lǎoshī.   I'm not a teacher.

                            jīnglǐ.   I'm not the manager.

                            zǒngjīnglǐ.   I'm not the general manager.

                            Zhōngguo rén.   I'm not Chinese.

5. **Nǐ**   jiào shémme míngzi?   What is your name?

   Tā   What is her name?

   Nǐ māma   What is your mother's name?

   Zhèiwèi tóngxué   What is this student's name?

   Nèiwèi lǎoshī   What is that teacher's name?

   Nǐ   What is your name?

6. Tā	jiào	shémme?	What is his name?
	wèn		What did he ask?
	bàn		What is he taking care of?
	yǒu		What does he have?
	jiào		What is his name?

7. Nǐmen dōu shi	Měiguo rén	ma?	Are you all Americans?
	lǎoshī		Are you all teachers?
	Rìběn rén		Are you all Japanese?
	Zhōngguo rén		Are you all Chinese?
	jīnglǐ		Are you all managers?
	Měiguo rén		Are you all Americans?

8. Wǒmen bù dōu shi	Měiguo rén.	We are not all Americans.
	Jiā'nádà rén.	We are not all Canadians.
	xīn lǎoshī.	We are not all new teachers.
	xuésheng.	We are not all students.
	zǒngjīnglǐ.	We are not all general managers.
	tóngshì.	We are not all colleagues.
	Měiguo rén.	We are not all Americans.

9. Wǒmen dōu bú shi	Měiguo rén.	None of us are Americans.
	Zhōngguo rén.	None of us are Chinese.
	Rìběn rén.	None of us are Japanese.
	lǎoshī.	None of us are teachers.
	jīnglǐ.	None of us are managers.
	háizi.	None of us are children.
	Měiguo rén.	None of us are Americans.

10. Nèiwèi	tóngxué	yě shi Rìběn rén.	That classmate is also Japanese.
	lǎoshī		That teacher is also Japanese.
	Gāo Xiānsheng		That Mr. Gao is also Japanese.
	Kē Tàitai		That Mrs. Ke is also Japanese.
	Lín Xiáojie		That Miss Lin is also Japanese.
	tóngxué		That classmate is also Japanese.

11. Něiwèi	tóngxué jiào Wáng Jīngshēng?	Which student is called Wang Jingsheng?
Zhèiwèi	.	This student is called Wang Jingsheng.
Nèiwèi	.	That student is called Wang Jingsheng.
Něiwèi	?	Which student is called Wang Jingsheng?

Unit 2, Part 2: Substitution Drills

Listen to the audio; after each prompt, say the new sentence using that substitution. Do each drill at least twice: first with the book open, then with the book closed. Each drill starts with a model sentence for you to repeat.

1. Zhè shi	wǒde	xīn tóngwū.	This is my new roommate.
	nǐde		This is your new roommate.
	tāde		This is her new roommate.
	Xiǎo Línde		This is Little Lin's new roommate.
	Lǎo Wángde		This is Old Wang's new roommate.
	wǒde		This is my new roommate.

2. Huānyíng nǐ dào	Zhōngguo	lái!	Welcome to China!
	wǒmende sùshè		Welcome to our dormitory!
	wǒmende shítáng		Welcome to our cafeteria!
	wǒmende túshūguǎn		Welcome to our library!
	Měiguo		Welcome to the United States!
	Rìběn		Welcome to Japan!
	Zhōngguo		Welcome to China!

3. Wǒ hěn gāoxing	rènshi nǐ.	I'm very happy to become acquainted with you.
	nǐ shi wǒde tóngwū.	I'm very happy that you are my roommate.
	nín shi wǒmende lǎoshī.	I'm very happy that you are our teacher.
	dào Zhōngguo qù.	I'm very happy to go to China.
	xuéxí Zhōngwén.	I'm very happy to study Chinese.
	dào Měiguo qù.	I'm very happy to go to the United States.
	rènshi nǐ.	I'm very happy to become acquainted with you.

4. Bié	zhèmme chēnghu wǒ!	Don't address me this way!
	wèn!	Don't ask!
	wèn ta!	Don't ask him!
	gāoxìng!	Don't be happy!
	bù gāoxìng!	Don't be unhappy!
	dào Zhōngguo qù!	Don't go to China!
	qù wǒmende sùshè!	Don't go to our dormitory!
	lái wǒmende shítáng!	Don't come to our dining hall!
	zhèmme chēnghu wǒ!	Don't address me this way!

5. Nǐ bú yào	zǒu!	Don't leave!
	qù!	Don't go!
	wèn!	Don't ask!
	lái!	Don't come!
	zuò!	Don't sit!
	zǒu!	Don't leave!

6. Háishi	jiào wǒ Xiǎo Chén	hǎole.	Why don't you just call me Little Chen.
	jiào wǒ Lǎo Luó		Why don't you just call me Old Luo.
	jiào tā Lín Tàitai		Why don't you just call her Mrs. Lin.
	dài nǐde tóngwū		Why don't you just bring your roommate.
	dài nǐde háizi		Why don't you just bring your kids.
	jiào wǒ Xiǎo Chén		Why don't you just call me Little Chen.

7. Wǒ yīnggāi zěmme chēnghu	nín?	How should I address you?
	nǐ?	How should I address you?
	tā?	How should I address him?
	nǐde tóngwū?	How should I address your roommate?
	nǐde bàba?	How should I address your father?
	nǐmende zǒngjīnglǐ?	How should I address your general manager?
	nín?	How should I address you?

8. Nà	shi shéi a?	Who is that?
Zhè		Who is this?
Tā		Who is she?
Tāmen		Who are they?
Nǐ		Who are you?
Nǐmen		Who are you all?
Wǒ		Who am I?
Wǒmen		Who are we?
Nà		Who is that?

Unit 2, Part 3: Substitution Drills

Listen to the audio; after each prompt, say the new sentence using that substitution. Do each drill at least twice first with the book open, then with the book closed. Each drill starts with a model sentence for you to repeat.

1. Wǒ xìng	Gāo.	Nín guìxìng?	My name is Gao. What is your name?
	Wáng.		My name is Wang. What is your name?
	Lín.		My name is Lin. What is your name?
	Shī.		My name is Shi. What is your name?
	Wú.		My name is Wu. What is your name?
	Chén.		My name is Chen. What is your name?
	Gāo.		My name is Gao. What is your name?

2. Nín zài něige	dānwèi	gōngzuò?	Which organization do you work at?
	gōngsī		Which company do you work at?
	dàxué		Which university do you work at?
	túshūguǎn		Which library do you work at?
	shítáng		Which cafeteria do you work at?
	dānwèi		Which organization do you work for?

3. Wǒ zài	Xiānggǎng Zhōngwén Dàxué	xuéxí.	I study at Chinese University of Hong Kong.
	sùshè		I study in the dormitory.
	túshūguǎn		I study at the library.
	shítáng		I study in the cafeteria.
	dānwèi		I study in my work unit.
	gōngsī		I study at the company.
	Xiānggǎng Zhōngwén Dàxué		I study at Chinese University of Hong Kong.

4. Xiǎo Wáng zài	něige	dàshǐguǎn gōngzuò?	Which embassy does Little Wang work at?
	zhèige	.	Little Wang works at this embassy
	nèige	.	Little Wang works at that embassy
	něige	?	Which embassy does Little Wang work at?

5. Tā bàba zài	yìjiā	gōngsī gōngzuò.	Her father works for a company.
	něijiā	?	Which company does her father work for?
	zhèijiā	.	Her father works for this company.
	nèijiā	.	Her father works for that company.
	yìjiā	.	Her father works for a company.

6. Nèiwèi	shi Mǎ Xiàozhǎng.	That is President Ma.
Zhèiwèi	.	This is President Ma.
Něiwèi	?	Which one is President Ma?
Nèiwèi	.	That is President Ma.

7. Tā shi nínde	xiānsheng	ba?	I suppose he is your husband?
	lǎoshī		I suppose he is your teacher?
	jīnglǐ		I suppose he is your manager?
	tàitai		I suppose she is your wife?
	tóngshì		I suppose she is your colleague?
	tóngwū		I suppose she is your roommate?
	tóngxué		I suppose she is your classmate?
	xiānsheng		I suppose he is your husband?

8. Nǐ hěn	gāoxìng	ba?	I suppose you must be happy?
	jǐnzhāng		I suppose you must be nervous?
	kùn		I suppose you must be sleepy?
	lèi		I suppose you must be tired?
	máng		I suppose you must be busy?
	gāoxìng		I suppose you must be happy?

9. Nǐmen yě	gōngzuò	ba?	I suppose you are also working?
	dài		I suppose you are also bringing some?
	rènshi		I suppose you are also acquainted?
	yǒu		I suppose you also have some?
	qù		I suppose you are also going?
	bàn		I suppose you are also doing it?
	gōngzuò		I suppose you are also working?

Unit 2, Part 4: Substitution Drills

Listen to the audio; after each prompt, say the new sentence using that substitution. Do each drill at least twic first with the book open, then with the book closed. Each drill starts with a model sentence for you to repeat.

1. Duìbuqǐ, wǒ méi	dài míngpiàn.	Sorry, I didn't bring a name card.
	jièshao tā.	Sorry, I didn't introduce him.
	wèn nǐ.	Sorry, I didn't ask you.
	xièxie nǐ.	Sorry, I didn't thank you.
	dài míngpiàn.	Sorry, I didn't bring a name card.

2. Wǒ gēn Luó Xiáojie dōu bú	shi Yīngguo rén.	Miss Luo and I, neither one of us is English.
	lèi.	Miss Luo and I, neither one of us is tired.
	kùn.	Miss Luo and I, neither one of us is sleepy.
	shi Měiguo rén.	Miss Luo and I, neither one of us is American.
	shi Zhōngguo rén.	Miss Luo and I, neither one of us is Chinese.
	shi Yīngguo rén.	Miss Luo and I, neither one of us is English.

3. Wǒ gēn Luó Xiáojie dōu bù	gāoxìng.	Miss Luo and I, neither one of us is happy.
	lái.	Miss Luo and I, neither one of us is coming.
	gāo.	Miss Luo and I, neither one of us is tall.
	lǎo.	Miss Luo and I, neither one of us is old.
	máng.	Miss Luo and I, neither one of us is busy.
	zǒu.	Miss Luo and I, neither one of us is leaving.
	gāoxìng.	Miss Luo and I, neither one of us is happy.

4. Tāmen dōu méi	qù.	None of them went.
	lái.	None of them came.
	zuò.	None of them sat.
	zǒu.	None of them left.
	wèn.	None of them asked.
	dài.	None of them brought it.
	gōngzuò.	None of them worked.
	qù.	None of them went.

5. Zhè shi	Zhōng-Měi Màoyì Gōngsī	de Shī Xiáojie.	This is Miss Shi from the Sino-American Trading Company.
	Xiānggǎng Dàxué		This is Miss Shi from Hong Kong University.
	Rìběn Dàshǐguǎn		This is Miss Shi from the Japanese Embassy.
	túshūguǎn		This is Miss Shi from the library.
	Jiā'nádà Dàshǐguǎn		This is Miss Shi from the Canadian Embassy.
	Zhōng-Měi Màoyì Gōngsī		This is Miss Shi from the Sino-American Trading Company.

6. Nǐ rènshi nèiwèi	**tàitai**	ma?	Do you know that lady?
	xiānsheng		Do you know that gentleman?
	xiáojie		Do you know that young lady?
	nǚshì		Do you know that lady?
	lǎoshī		Do you know that teacher?
	xiàozhǎng		Do you know that president?
	tóngxué		Do you know that classmate?
	tàitai		Do you know that lady?

7. Nǐ dài bu dài	**míngpiàn?**	Are you bringing name cards?
	tóngxué?	Are you bringing classmates?
	tóngshì?	Are you bringing colleagues?
	nǐ xiānsheng?	Are you bringing your husband?
	nǐ tàitai?	Are you bringing your wife?
	nǐ māma?	Are you bringing your mother?
	nǐde háizi?	Are you bringing your children?
	Gāo Xiáojie?	Are you bringing Miss Gao?
	míngpiàn?	Are you bringing name cards?

8. Tāmen méi dōu	**qù.**	Not all of them went.
	zuò.	Not all of them sat.
	zǒu.	Not all of them left.
	wèn.	Not all of them asked.
	lái.	Not all of them came.
	qù.	Not all of them went.

. . . .

Unit 3, Part 1: Substitution Drills

Listen to the audio; after each prompt, say the new sentence using that substitution. Do each drill at least twice first with the book open, then with the book closed. Each drill starts with a model sentence for you to repeat.

1. Tāmen bānshang yǒu	jǐge	tóngxué?	How many classmates are there in their class?
	yíge	.	There is one classmate in their class.
	liǎngge	.	There are two classmates in their class.
	sān'ge	.	There are three classmates in their class.
	sìge	.	There are four classmates in their class.
	wǔge	.	There are five classmates in their class.
	liùge	.	There are six classmates in their class.
	qíge	.	There are seven classmates in their class.
	báge	.	There are eight classmates in their class.
	jiǔge	.	There are nine classmates in their class.
	shíge	.	There are ten classmates in their class.
	jǐge	?	How many classmates are there in their class?

2. Bānshang	yǒu shíge rén.	In the class there are ten people.
Túshūguǎn		In the library there are ten people.
Sùshè		In the dormitory there are ten people.
Shítáng		In the dining hall there are ten people.
Gōngsī		In the company there are ten people.
Dānwèi		In the organization there are ten people.
Bānshang		In the class there are ten people.

3. Tāmen yǒu	jǐwèi	lǎoshī?	How many teachers do they have?
	yíwèi	.	They have one teacher.
	liǎngwèi	.	They have two teachers.
	sānwèi	.	They have three teachers.
	sìwèi	.	They have four teachers.
	wǔwèi	.	They have five teachers.
	liùwèi	.	They have six teachers.
	qíwèi	.	They have seven teachers.
	báwèi	.	They have eight teachers.
	jiǔwèi	.	They have nine teachers.
	shíwèi	.	They have ten teachers.
	jǐwèi	?	How many teachers do they have?

4. **Yígòng yǒu**

sānwèi.	In all, there are three of them.
sān'ge.	In all, there are three.
sān'ge rén.	In all, there are three people.
sān'ge nánshēng.	In all, there are three male students.
sān'ge nǔshēng.	In all, there are three female students.
sān'ge nánde.	In all, there are three men.
sān'ge nǔde.	In all, there are three women.
sān'ge háizi.	In all, there are three children.
sān'ge bān.	In all, there are three class sections.
sān'ge shítáng.	In all, there are three cafeterias.
sānwèi Zhào Xiáojie.	In all, there are three Miss Zhaos.
sānwèi nánlǎoshī.	In all, there are three male teachers.
sānwèi nǔlǎoshī.	In all, there are three female teachers.
sānwèi.	In all, there are three of them.

Unit 3, Part 2: Substitution Drills

Listen to the audio; after each prompt, say the new sentence using that substitution. Do each drill at least twice, first with the book open, then with the book closed. Each drill starts with a model sentence for you to repeat.

1. **Tā**   duō dà niánji le?   How old is she?

   Tāde háizi   How old is her child?

   Lǎo Gāo   How old is Old Gao?

   Tāmen   How old are they?

   Nèiwèi lǎoshī   How old is that teacher?

   Wáng Xiáojie   How old is Ms. Wang?

   Tā   How old is she?

2. **Nǐ mèimei**   jǐsuì le?   How old is your younger sister?

   Nǐ dìdi   How old is your younger brother?

   Zhèige háizi   How old is this child?

   Nèige háizi   How old is that child?

   Nǐde háizi   How old is your child?

   Nǐ   How old are you?

   Nǐmen   How old are you?

   Nǐ mèimei   How old is your younger sister?

3. Wǒ jīnnián   **èrshi'èr**   suì le. I'm twenty-two this year.

                     shíliù   I'm sixteen this year.

                     shíqī   I'm seventeen this year.

                     shíbā   I'm eighteen this year.

                     shíjiǔ   I'm nineteen this year.

                     èrshí   I'm twenty this year.

                     èrshiyī   I'm twenty-one this year.

                     èrshi'èr   I'm twenty-two this year.

4. Nǐ   **xiángxiang**   kàn.   Try to think.

                     wènwen   Try to ask.

                     zuòzuo   Try to sit.

                     cāicai   Try to guess.

                     jiàojiao   Try to call (somebody's name).

                     xiángxiang   Try to think.

5. Zhè shi nǐ   **mèimei**   , duì bu duì?   This is your younger sister, right?

                     dìdi   This is your younger brother, right?

                     gēge   This is your older brother, right?

                     jiějie   This is your older sister, right?

                     fùqin   This is your father, right?

                     mǔqin   This is your mother, right?

                     àirén   This is your spouse, right?

                     mèimei   This is your younger sister, right?

6. Nǐ bié	**kàn**	, hǎo bu hǎo?	Don't look, O.K.?
	wèn		Don't ask, O.K.?
	lái		Don't come, O.K.?
	qù		Don't go, O.K.?
	zuò		Don't sit down, O.K.?
	zǒu		Don't leave, O.K.?
	cāi		Don't guess, O.K.?
	kàn		Don't look, O.K.?

7. Nǐ dìdi hěn	**kě'ài!**		Your younger brother is cute!
	gāo!		Your younger brother is tall!
	ǎi!		Your younger brother is short!
	dà!		Your younger brother is big!
	xiǎo!		Your younger brother is small!
	hǎo!		Your younger brother is good!
	gāoxìng!		Your younger brother is happy!
	máng!		Your younger brother is busy!
	kùn!		Your younger brother is sleepy!
	kě'ài!		Your younger brother is cute!

8. Tā xiàge yuè jiù	**jiǔsuì**	le.	She will be nine years old next month.
	èrshiyīsuì		She will be twenty-one years old next month.
	lái		She will come next month.
	bù lái		She will not come next month.
	yǒu		She will have it next month.
	méiyou		She will not have it next month.
	yǒu háizi		She will have a child next month.
	zǒu		She will leave next month.
	jiǔsuì		She will be nine years old next month.

Unit 3, Part 3: Substitution Drills

Listen to the audio; after each prompt, say the new sentence using that substitution. Do each drill at least twice first with the book open, then with the book closed. Each drill starts with a model sentence for you to repeat.

1. **Qǐng wèn,**	**zhèige**	duōshǎo qián?	Excuse me, how much is this?
	zhèige bēibāo		Excuse me, how much is this backpack?
	nèige		Excuse me, how much is that?
	nèige bēibāo		Excuse me, how much is that backpack?
	bēizi		Excuse me, how much is that cup?
	gōngshìbāo		Excuse me, how much is that briefcase?
	yíge yuè		Excuse me, how much is it for a month?
	liǎngge yuè		Excuse me, how much is it for two months?
	zhèige		Excuse me, how much is this?

2. **Yò, tài**	**guì**	le.	Gosh, that's too expensive.
	dà		Gosh, that's too big.
	xiǎo		Gosh, that's too small.
	cháng		Gosh, that's too long.
	nán		Gosh, that's too hard.
	guì		Gosh, that's too expensive.

3. **Nèige zhǐ yào**	**sānkuài wǔ.**	That is only three dollars and fifty cents.
	yìfēn qián.	That is only one cent.
	liùkuài wǔ.	That is only six dollars and fifty cents.
	shíkuài qián.	That is only ten dollars.
	jiǔqiān jiǔbǎi jiǔshijiǔkuài.	That is only nine thousand nine hundred and ninety-nine dollars.
	qīkuài sì.	That is only seven dollars and forty cents.
	sānkuài wǔ.	That is only three dollars and fifty cents.

4. **Wǒ kànkan,**	**xíng bu xíng?**	Let me see, O.K.?
	xíng ma?	Let me see, O.K.?
	hǎo bu hǎo?	Let me see, O.K.?
	hǎo ma?	Let me see, O.K.?
	xíng bu xíng?	Let me see, O.K.?

5. **Qǐng nǐ**	**kànkan.**	Please take a look.
	wènwen.	Please go and ask.
	zuòzuo.	Please sit down.
	xiángxiang.	Please think about it.
	cāicai.	Please guess.
	kànkan.	Please take a look.

6. Nín	kàn	ba.	Why don't you look.
	cāi		Why don't you guess.
	wèn		Why don't you ask.
	mǎi		Why don't you buy it.
	mài		Why don't you sell it.
	zuò		Why don't you sit.
	zǒu		Why don't you leave.
	lái		Why don't you come.
	qù		Why don't you go.
	kàn		Why don't you look.

7. Wǒmen	zǒu	ba.	Let's leave.
	huí sùshè		Let's return to the dormitory.
	qù túshūguǎn		Let's go to the library.
	yě dài míngpiàn		Let's also bring name cards.
	yě xuéxí Zhōngwén		Let's also study Chinese.
	yě jiào tā Xiǎo Mǎ		Let's also call him Little Ma.
	yě mǎi yíge		Let's also buy one.
	zǒu		Let's leave.

8. Wǒ méi dài	míngpiàn.		I didn't bring name cards.
	qián.		I didn't bring money.
	gōngzuò.		I didn't bring work.
	bēizi.		I didn't bring a cup.
	dàizi.		I didn't bring a bag.
	bēibāo.		I didn't bring a backpack.
	gōngshìbāo.		I didn't bring a briefcase.
	míngpiàn.		I didn't bring name cards.

Unit 3, Part 4: Substitution Drills

Listen to the audio; after each prompt, say the new sentence using that substitution. Do each drill at least twice first with the book open, then with the book closed. Each drill starts with a model sentence for you to repeat.

1. **Xià yítàng dào**

Tiānjīn	**de huǒchē jǐdiǎn kāi?**	When does the next train for Tianjin depart?
Yīngguó		When does the next train for England depart?
Fǎguó		When does the next train for France depart?
Déguó		When does the next train for Germany depart?
Xībānyá		When does the next train for Spain depart?
Měiguó		When does the next train for the U.S. depart?
Jiā'nádà		When does the next train for Canada depart?
Zhōngguó		When does the next train for China depart?
Tiānjīn		When does the next train for Tianjin depart?

2. **Xià yítàng dào Tiānjīn**   de huǒchē jǐdiǎn kāi?   When does the next train for Tianjin depart?

Bādiǎn èrshí dào Tiānjīn	When does the train that arrives in Tianjin at 8:20 depart?
Shí'èrdiǎn dào Xīnjiāpō	When does the train that arrives in Singapore at 12:00 depart?
Wǒ gēn Bái Tàitai zuò	When does the train that Mrs. Bai and I are taking depart?
Tāmen yīnggāi zuò	When does the train that they're supposed to take depart?
Lǎo Chén děi zuò	When does the train that Old Chen must take depart?
Xià yítàng dào Tiānjīn	When does the next train for Tianjin depart?

3. **Tā**

yīdiǎn	**èrshí dào.**	She arrives at 1:20.
liǎngdiǎn		She arrives at 2:20.
sāndiǎn		She arrives at 3:20.
sìdiǎn		She arrives at 4:20.
wǔdiǎn		She arrives at 5:20.
liùdiǎn		She arrives at 6:20.
qīdiǎn		She arrives at 7:20.
bādiǎn		She arrives at 8:20.
jiǔdiǎn		She arrives at 9:20.
shídiǎn		She arrives at 10:20.
shíyīdiǎn		She arrives at 11:20.
shí'èrdiǎn		She arrives at 12:20.
yīdiǎn		She arrives at 1:20.

4. Jiŭdiăn	èrshí.	9:20.
	bàn.	9:30.
	sānkè.	9:45.
	wŭshí.	9:50.
	wŭfēn.	9:05.
	shífēn.	9:10.
	yíkè.	9:15.
	èrshí.	9:20.

5. Kŏngpà nín	láibujíle.	I'm afraid you're not going to make it.
	găocuòle.	I'm afraid you got it wrong.
	lèile.	I'm afraid you're tired.
	kùnle.	I'm afraid you've gotten sleepy.
	dĕi zŏule.	I'm afraid you have to go now.
	láibujíle.	I'm afraid you're not going to make it.

6. Nà, wŏ jiù zuò	shídiăn bàn de.	In that case, I'll take the 10:30 one.
	liùdiăn yíkè	In that case, I'll take the 6:15 one.
	qīdiăn sānkè	In that case, I'll take the 7:45 one.
	bādiăn wŭfēn	In that case, I'll take the 8:05 one.
	jiŭdiăn èrshí	In that case, I'll take the 9:20 one.
	wŭdiăn bàn	In that case, I'll take the 5:30 one.
	sìdiăn yíkè	In that case, I'll take the 4:15 one.
	shídiăn bàn	In that case, I'll take the 10:30 one.

7. Dào	Tiānjīn yào duō cháng shíjiān?	How long does it take to get to Tianjin?
	Făguo	How long does it take to get to France?
	túshūguăn	How long does it take to get to the library?
	shítáng	How long does it take to get to the cafeteria?
	sùshè	How long does it take to get to the dormitory?
	Déguo	How long does it take to get to Germany?
	Tiānjīn	How long does it take to get to Tianjin?

8. Chàbuduō yào	liăngge bàn zhōngtóu.	It takes about two and a half hours.
	bàn'ge	It takes about half an hour.
	yíge bàn	It takes about one and a half hours.
	sān'ge bàn	It takes about three and a half hours.
	yíge	It takes about one hour.
	qīge bàn	It takes about seven and a half hours.
	liăngge bàn	It takes about two and a half hours.

Unit 4, Part 1: Substitution Drills

Listen to the audio; after each prompt, say the new sentence using that substitution. Do each drill at least twice, first with the book open, then with the book closed. Each drill starts with a model sentence for you to repeat.

1. Qǐng wèn,	yǔyán shíyànshì	jǐdiǎn zhōng kāimén?	Excuse me, what time does the language lab open?
	túshūguǎn		Excuse me, what time does the library open?
	shítáng		Excuse me, what time does the cafeteria open?
	dàshǐguǎn		Excuse me, what time does the embassy open?
	màoyì gōngsī		Excuse me, what time does the trading company open?
	shíyànshì		Excuse me, what time does the laboratory open?
	yǔyán shíyànshì		Excuse me, what time does the language lab open?

2. Qǐng wèn,	yǔyán shíyànshì	jǐdiǎn zhōng guānmén?	Excuse me, what time does the language lab close?
	túshūguǎn		Excuse me, what time does the library close?
	shítáng		Excuse me, what time does the cafeteria close?
	dàshǐguǎn		Excuse me, what time does the embassy close?
	màoyì gōngsī		Excuse me, what time does the trading company close?
	shíyànshì		Excuse me, what time does the laboratory close?
	yǔyán shíyànshì		Excuse me, what time does the language lab close?

3. Měitiān zǎoshang	bādiǎn	kāimén.	It opens at 8:00 A.M. every day.
	qīdiǎn bàn		It opens at 7:30 A.M. every day.
	shídiǎn yíkè		It opens at 10:15 A.M. every day.
	liùdiǎn bàn		It opens at 6:30 A.M. every day.
	jiǔdiǎn sānkè		It opens at 9:45 A.M. every day.
	shídiǎn wǔfēn		It opens at 10:05 A.M. every day.
	bādiǎn		It opens at 8:00 A.M. every day.

4. Wǎnshang	jiǔdiǎn bàn	guānmén.	It closes at 9:30 P.M.
	shídiǎn bàn		It closes at 10:30 P.M.
	bādiǎn yíkè		It closes at 8:15 P.M.
	liùdiǎn sānkè		It closes at 6:45 P.M.
	qīdiǎn		It closes at 7:00 P.M.
	jiǔdiǎn bàn		It closes at 9:30 P.M.

5. **Xīngqīliù**   kāi bu kāi?   Is it open on Saturday?

   Xīnqīyī   Is it open on Monday?

   Xīngqī'èr   Is it open on Tuesday?

   Xīngqīsān   Is it open on Wednesday?

   Xīngqīsì   Is it open on Thursday?

   Xīngqīwǔ   Is it open on Friday?

   Xīngqītiān   Is it open on Sunday?

   Xīngqīrì   Is it open on Sunday?

   Xīngqīliù   Is is open on Saturday?

---

6. **Lǐbàiliù**   kāi bàntiān.   It's open half-days on Saturday.

   Lǐbàiyī   It's open half-days on Monday.

   Lǐbài'èr   It's open half-days on Tuesday.

   Lǐbàisān   It's open half-days on Wednesday.

   Lǐbàisì   It's open half-days on Thursday.

   Lǐbàiwǔ   It's open half-days on Friday.

   Lǐbàitiān   It's open half-days on Sunday.

   Lǐbàirì   It's open half-days on Sunday.

   Lǐbàiliù   It's open half-days on Saturday.

---

7. **Xīngqītiān**   xiūxi.   He rests on Sundays.

   Zǎoshang   It's closed in the morning.

   Wǎnshang   It's closed in the evening.

   Shàngwǔ   It's closed mornings.

   Xiàwǔ   It's closed afternoons.

   Shàngge xīngqī   It was closed last week.

   Zhèige xīngqī   It's closed this week.

   Xiàge xīngqī   It's closed next week.

   Píngcháng   It's ordinarily closed.

   Měitiān dōu   It's closed every day.

   Xīngqītiān   He rests on Sundays.

---

8. Wǒ píngcháng zǎoshàng   **qīdiǎn**   qǐchuáng.   I usually get up from bed at 7:00.

                           wǔdiǎn bàn   I usually get up from bed at 5:30.

                           liùdiǎn yíkè   I usually get up from bed at 6:15.

                           bādiǎn bàn   I usually get up from bed at 8:30.

                           jiǔdiǎn sānkè   I usually get up from bed at 9:45.

                           qīdiǎn èrshí   I usually get up from bed at 7:20.

                           qīdiǎn   I usually get up from bed at 7:00.

9. Wǒ píngcháng	shíyīdiǎn zhōng	shuìjiào.	I usually go to bed at 11:00.
	liǎngdiǎn bàn		I usually go to bed at 2:30.
	shídiǎn yíkè		I usually go to bed at 10:15.
	shí'èrdiǎn sānkè		I usually go to bed at 12:45.
	sāndiǎn zhōng		I usually go to bed at 3:00.
	yīdiǎn bàn		I usually go to bed at 1:30.
	liǎngdiǎn yíkè		I usually go to bed at 2:15.
	shíyīdiǎn		I usually go to bed at 11:00.

10. Wǒ píngcháng měitiān shuì	qíge	zhōngtóu.	I usually sleep for seven hours every day.
	báge		I usually sleep for eight hours every day.
	liùge bàn		I usually sleep for six and a half hours every day.
	sìge		I usually sleep for four hours every day.
	wǔge bàn		I usually sleep for five and a half hours every day.
	shí'èrge		I usually sleep for twelve hours every day.
	shíge		I usually sleep for ten hours every day.
	qíge		I usually sleep for seven hours every day.

Unit 4, Part 2: Substitution Drills

Listen to the audio; after each prompt, say the new sentence using that substitution. Do each drill at least twice: first with the book open, then with the book closed. Each drill starts with a model sentence for you to repeat.

1. **Nǐ**   jiào shémme míngzi?   What is your name?

   Tā   What is her name?

   Nǐ àirén   What is your spouse's name?

   Nǐde háizi   What is your child's name?

   Nǐde tóngwū   What is your roommate's name?

   Nǐde tóngxué   What is your classmate's name?

   Nèiwèi tóngshì   What is that colleague's name?

   Nǐ   What is your name?

2. **Nǐ**   shi něinián chūshēngde?   In what year were you born?

   Tā   In what year was she born?

   Gāo Xiānsheng   In what year was Mr. Gao born?

   Bái Xiáojie   In what year was Ms. Bai born?

   Lǎo Wáng   In what year was Old Wang born?

   Xiǎo Lín   In what year was Little Lin born?

   Tāmen   In what year were they born?

   Chén Tàitai   In what year was Mrs. Chen born?

   Nǐ   In what year were you born?

3. Wǒ shi   **yī-jiǔ-qī-jiǔ-nián**   chūshēngde.   I was born in 1979.

                   yī-jiǔ-bā-líng-nián   I was born in 1980.

                   yī-jiǔ-bā-yī-nián   I was born in 1981.

                   yī-jiǔ-bā-èr-nián   I was born in 1982.

                   yī-jiǔ-jiǔ-sān-nián   I was born in 1993.

                   yī-jiǔ-jiǔ-sì-nián   I was born in 1994.

                   yī-jiǔ-jiǔ-wǔ-nián   I was born in 1995.

                   yī-jiǔ-qī-jiǔ-nián   I was born in 1979.

4. Wǒde shēngrì shi   **sìyuè shísānhào.**   My birthday is April 13th.

                       shíyuè yīhào.   My birthday is October 1st.

                       sānyuè èrshibāhào.   My birthday is March 28th.

                       jiǔyuè sìhào.   My birthday is September 4th.

                       liùyuè èrshihào.   My birthday is June 20th

                       wǔyuè sānhào.   My birthday is May 3rd.

                       yīyuè sānshihào.   My birthday is January 30th.

                       sìyuè shísānhào.   My birthday is April 13th.

5. **Wénhuà Lù**

sìhào		4 Culture Road
sānbǎi èrshisānhào		323 Culture Road
bābǎi líng wǔhào		805 Culture Road
shísānhào		13 Culture Road
sānshihào		30 Culture Road
jiǔhào		9 Culture Road
sìbǎi wǔshiwǔhào		455 Culture Road
sìhào		4 Culture Road

6. **Hépíng Dōng Lù**

yī	**duàn sìhào.**	Number 4, Hoping East Road Section One.
èr		Number 4, Hoping East Road Section Two.
sān		Number 4, Hoping East Road Section Three.
sì		Number 4, Hoping East Road Section Four.
wǔ		Number 4, Hoping East Road Section Five.
liù		Number 4, Hoping East Road Section Six.
qī		Number 4, Hoping East Road Section Seven.
yī		Number 4, Hoping East Road Section One.

7. **Tiānjīn Lù**

èrxiàng	**qīhào.**	Number 7, Lane 2, Tianjin Road.
yīxiàng		Number 7, Lane 1, Tianjin Road.
sānxiàng		Number 7, Lane 3, Tianjin Road.
sìxiàng		Number 7, Lane 4, Tianjin Road.
wǔxiàng		Number 7, Lane 5, Tianjin Road.
liùxiàng		Number 7, Lane 6, Tianjin Road.
qīxiàng		Number 7, Lane 7, Tianjin Road.
èrxiàng		Number 7, Lane 2, Tianjin Road.

8. **Tā yào qù**

jǐlóu?	What floor does she want to go to?
yīlóu.	She wants to go to the first floor.
èrlóu.	She wants to go to the second floor.
sānlóu.	She wants to go to the third floor.
sìlóu.	She wants to go to the fourth floor.
wǔlóu.	She wants to go to the fifth floor.
liùlóu.	She wants to go to the sixth floor.
qīlóu.	She wants to go to the seventh floor.
jǐlóu?	What floor does she want to go to?

9. Qǐng	nǐ	děng yíxià.	Could you wait a moment, please?
	tā		Could she wait a moment, please?
	tāmen		Could they wait a moment, please?
	Zhào Xiānsheng		Could Mr. Zhao wait a moment, please?
	Xiè Tàitai		Could Mrs. Xie wait a moment, please?
	Wáng Xiáojie		Could Miss Wang wait a moment, please?
	Lǎo Zhāng		Could Old Zhang wait a moment, please?
	Xiǎo Mǎ		Could Little Ma wait a moment, please?
	nǐ		Could you wait a moment, please?

10. Jīntiān	jǐyuè jǐhào?	What is today's date?
Míngtiān		What is tomorrow's date?
Zuótiān		What was yesterday's date?
Jīnnián		Which month and which day this year?
Míngnián		Which month and which day next year?
Qùnián		Which month and which day last year?
Nǐde shēngrì		When is your birthday?
Jīntiān		What is today's date?

11. Jīnnián	shi něinián?	What year is this year?
Míngnián		What year will it be next year?
Qùnián		What year was it last year?
Jīnnián		What year is this year?

· ·

Unit 4, Part 3: Substitution Drills

Listen to the audio; after each prompt, say the new sentence using that substitution. Do each drill at least twice first with the book open, then with the book closed. Each drill starts with a model sentence for you to repeat.

1. Zhè shi tā dì	jǐ	cì dào Zhōngguo lái?	How many times has he been to China?
	yī	.	This is his first time in China.
	èr	.	This is his second time in China.
	sān	.	This is his third time in China.
	sì	.	This is his fourth time in China.
	wǔ	.	This is his fifth time in China.
	liù	.	This is his sixth time in China.
	qī	.	This is his seventh time in China.
	bā	.	This is his eighth time in China.
	jiǔ	.	This is his ninth time in China.
	jǐ	?	How many times has he been to China?

2. Zhè shi wǒ dì	èr	cì lái.	This is my second time here.
	yī		This is my first time here.
	sān		This is my third time here.
	sì		This is my fourth time here.
	wǔ		This is my fifth time here.
	liù		This is my sixth time here.
	qī		This is my seventh time here.
	bā		This is my eighth time here.
	jiǔ		This is my ninth time here.
	èr		This is my second time here.

3. Dì	yí	ge rén shi shéi?	Who was the first person?
	èr		Who was the second person?
	sān		Who was the third person?
	sì		Who was the fourth person?
	wǔ		Who was the fifth person?
	liù		Who was the sixth person?
	qī		Who was the seventh person?
	bā		Who was the eighth person?
	jiǔ		Who was the ninth person?
	shí		Who was the tenth person?
	yí		Who was the first person?

4. Yǒu yìsi, dì	èr	wèi lǎoshī yě xìng Wáng!	Interesting, the 2nd teacher's surname was also Wang!
	sān		Interesting, the 3rd teacher's surname was also Wang!
	sì		Interesting, the 4th teacher's surname was also Wang!
	wǔ		Interesting, the 5th teacher's surname was also Wang!
	liù		Interesting, the 6th teacher's surname was also Wang!
	qī		Interesting, the 7th teacher's surname was also Wang!
	bā		Interesting, the 8th teacher's surname was also Wang!
	èr		Interesting, the 2nd teacher's surname was also Wang!

5. Wǒ	lái	guo.	I've been here before.
	qù		I've been there before.
	wèn		I've asked before.
	mǎi		I've bought them before.
	mài		I've sold them before.
	lái		I've been here before.

6. Tā láiguo	yí	cì.	She has been here once.
	liǎng	.	She has been here twice.
	sān	.	She has been here three times.
	sì	.	She has been here four times.
	wǔ	.	She has been here five times.
	liù	.	She has been here six times.
	qī	.	She has been here seven times.
	bā	.	She has been here eight times.
	jiǔ	.	She has been here nine times.
	shí	.	She has been here ten times
	jǐ	?	How many times has she been here?
	yí	.	She has been here once.

7. Lǎo Zhào méi	zuò	guo.	Old Zhao has never taken one (e.g., a train) before.
	mǎi		Old Zhao has never bought one before.
	mài		Old Zhao has never sold one before.
	shuō		Old Zhao has never said it before.
	zuò		Old Zhao has never taken one before.

8.	Tā zhèicì yào zhù	**duō jiǔ?**		How long will he stay this time?
		liǎngtiān.		He will stay for two days this time.
		liǎngge xīngqī.		He will stay for two weeks this time.
		liǎngge yuè.		He will stay for two months this time.
		liǎngnián.		He will stay for two years this time.
		bàn'ge yuè.		He will stay for half a month this time.
		yíge bàn yuè.		He will stay for one and a half months this time.
		duō jiǔ?		How long will he stay this time?

9.	Wǒ míngtiān huí	**guó.**	I'll return to my native country tomorrow.
		jiā.	I'll go home tomorrow.
		sùshè.	I'll return to my dorm tomorrow.
		xuéxiào.	I'll return to school tomorrow.
		guó.	I'll return to my native country tomorrow.

10.	Nǐ zhù	**něige**	**fángjiān?**	In which room are you staying?
		jǐhào		What is the number of the room in which you are staying?
		shéide		Whose room are you staying in?
		něige		In which room are you staying?

11.	Tā zhù	**sān líng liù.**	She is staying in 306.
		èr jiǔ bā.	She is staying in 298.
		sùshè.	She is staying in the dormitory.
		wǒ jiā.	She is staying in my home.
		něige fángjiān?	Which room is she staying in?
		wǒde fángjiān.	She is staying in my room.
		nǎr?	Where is she staying?
		sān líng liù.	She is staying in 306.

12.	Tā xiān	**shuōle**	shémme? Ránhòu	**shuōle**	shémme?	What did he say first? What did he say then?
		zuòle		**zuòle**		What did he do first? What did he do then?
		wènle		**wènle**		What did he ask first? What did he ask then?
		mǎile		**mǎile**		What did he buy first? What did he buy then?
		kànle		**kànle**		What did he look at first? What did he look at then?
		shuōle		**shuōle**		What did he say first? What did he say then?

13.	Nǐ shì bu shi	**qiántiān**	láiguo wǒ jiā?	Did you come to my house the day before yesterday?
		zuótiān		Did you come to my house yesterday?
		jīntiān shàngwǔ		Did you come to my house this morning?
		qiánnián		Did you come to my house the year before last?
		qùnián		Did you come to my house last year?
		jīnnián èryuè		Did you come to my house February of this year?
		qiántiān		Did you come to my house the day before yesterday?

14. **Bái Xiānsheng shuō tā** | **jīnnián** | **bù huíguó.** | Mr. Bai says he won't return to his country this year.
| | **míngnián** | | Mr. Bai says he won't return to his country next year.
| | **hòunián** | | Mr. Bai says he won't return to his country the year after next.
| | **xiàge yuè** | | Mr. Bai says he won't return to his country next month.
| | **xiàge xīngqī** | | Mr. Bai says he won't return to his country next week.
| | **míngtiān** | | Mr. Bai says he won't return to his country tomorrow.
| | **hòutiān** | | Mr. Bai says he won't return to his country the day after tomorrow.
| | **jīnnián** | | Mr. Bai says he won't return to his country this year.

For the remaining pages of Substitution Drills
(**Unit 4, Part 4** through **Unit 10, Part 4**),
please refer to the disc.

For the remaining pages of Substitution Drills
(**Unit 4, Part 4** through **Unit 10, Part 4**),
please refer to the disc.

3. Transformation and Response Drills

Unit 1, Part 1: Transformation and Response Drills

1. Add the final particle **a** to the following greetings and questions to make them softer and more colloquial.

Nǐ hǎo!

"How are you?"

Nǐ hǎo a?

"How are you?"

Wāng Jīngshēng, nǐ hǎo!

"Wang Jingsheng, how are you?"

Wāng Jīngshēng, nǐ hǎo a!

"Wang Jingsheng, how are you?"

Nǐ dào nǎr qù?

"Where are you going?"

Nǐ dào nǎr qù a?

"Where are you going?"

Kē Léi'ēn dào nǎr qù bàn shì?

"Where is Ke Leien going to take care of things?"

Kē Léi'ēn dào nǎr qù bàn shì a?

"Where is Ke Leien going to take care of things?"

2. Use **ne** to abbreviate the question about the second person.

Wǒ huí sùshè. Nǐ dào nǎr qù?

"I'm going back to the dormitory. Where are you going?"

Wǒ huí sùshè. Nǐ ne?

"I'm going back to the dormitory. How about you?"

Wǒ qù bàn yìdiǎnr shì. Nǐ dào nǎr qù?

"I'm going to go take care of some stuff. Where are you going?"

Wǒ qù bàn yìdiǎnr shì. Nǐ ne?

"I'm going to go take care of some stuff. And you?"

Wǒ qù shítáng. Nǐ dào nǎr qù?

"I'm going to the cafeteria. Where are you going?"

Wǒ qù shítáng. Nǐ ne?

"I'm going to the cafeteria. And how about you?"

Wǒ qù túshūguǎn. Nǐ dào nǎr qù?

"I'm going to the library. Where are you going?"

Wǒ qù túshūguǎn. Nǐ ne?

"I'm going to the library. And you?"

3. You will hear a statement about somebody who is going to do something. Repeat the statement and, using the adverb **yě** "also, too," add a comment to the effect that you are going to do the same thing as the person being talked about.

Kē Léi'ēn huí sùshè.

"Ke Leien is returning to the dormitory."

Kē Léi'ēn huí sùshè, wǒ yě huí sùshè.

"Ke Leien is returning to the dormitory, and I'm returning to the dormitory, too."

Wāng Jīngshēng qù shítáng.

"Wang Jingsheng is going to the cafeteria."

Wāng Jīngshēng qù shítáng, wǒ yě qù shítáng.

"Wang Jingsheng is going to the cafeteria, and I'm going to the cafeteria, too."

Nǐ qù túshūguǎn.

"You're going to the library."

Nǐ qù túshūguǎn, wǒ yě qù túshūguǎn.

"You're going to the library, and I'm going to the library, too."

Nǐ qù bàn yìdiǎnr shì.

"You're going to go take care of some things."

Nǐ qù bàn yìdiǎnr shì, wǒ yě qù bàn yìdiǎnr shì.

"You're going to go take care of some things, and I'm going to go take care of some things, too."

Unit 1, Part 2: Transformation and Response Drills

1. Add **dōu** to each sentence.

   Wǒ bàba, māma hěn máng.

   "My father and mother are busy."

   Wǒ bàba, māma dōu hěn máng.

   "My father and mother are both busy."

   Wǒ àirén, háizi qù túshūguǎn.

   "My spouse and children go to the library."

   Wǒ àirén, háizi dōu qù túshūguǎn.

   "My spouse and children all go to the library."

   Tāmen xiān zǒule.

   "They left early."

   Tāmen dōu xiān zǒule.

   "They all left early."

   Nǐ bàba, māma hěn lèi.

   "Your father and mother are tired."

   Nǐ bàba, māma dōu hěn lèi.

   "Your father and mother are both tired."

2. Change the following statements into questions by adding the question particle **ma**.

   Tāmen hěn máng.

   "They are busy."

   Tāmen hěn máng ma?

   "Are they very busy?"

   Nǐ lèile.

   "You've gotten tired."

   Nǐ lèile ma?

   "Have you gotten tired?"

   Tāmen qù túshūguǎn.

   "They're going to the library."

   Tāmen qù túshūguǎn ma?

   "Are they going to the library?"

   Tā huí sùshè.

   "She's going back to the dormitory."

   Tā huí sùshè ma?

   "Is she going back to the dormitory?"

   Wǒ àirén xiān zǒule.

   "My spouse left already."

   Wǒ àirén xiān zǒule ma?

   "Did my spouse leave already?"

   Tā hái hǎo.

   "He's O.K."

   Tā hái hǎo ma?

   "Is he O.K.?"

3. Create stative verb sentences with **hěn** using the subjects and stative verbs given you.

   Nǐmen, lèi.

   "You (plural), tired."

   Nǐmen hěn lèi.

   "You are very tired."

   Tā, máng.

   "She, busy."

   Tā hěn máng.

   "She is very busy."

   Wǒ, hǎo.

   "I, good."

   Wǒ hěn hǎo.

   "I am doing very well."

   Nǐ, máng.

   "You, busy."

   Nǐ hěn máng.

   "You are very busy."

   Tāmen, lèi.

   "They, tired."

   Tāmen hěn lèi.

   "They are very tired."

4. Change the pronoun subject **tā** to the plural by adding **-men**.

Tā qù túshūguǎn.

"He's going to the library."

Tā huí sùshè.

"She's going back to the dormitory."

Tā hěn máng.

"He is very busy."

Tā xiān zǒule.

"She left earlier."

Tāmen qù túshūguǎn.

"They're going to the library."

Tāmen huí sùshè.

"They're going back to the dormitory."

Tāmen hěn máng.

"They are very busy."

Tāmen xiān zǒule.

"They left earlier."

· ·

Unit 1, Part 3: Transformation and Response Drills

1. Change the following from the pattern NOUN + STATIVE VERB to the pattern STATIVE VERB USED AS AN ADJECTIVE + NOUN.

Gōngzuò hǎo.	**hǎo gōngzuò**
"The job is good."	"good job"
Háizi xiǎo.	**xiǎo háizi**
"The child is little."	"little child"
Bàba hǎo.	**hǎo bàba**
"Father is good."	"good father"
Shítáng hǎo.	**hǎo shítáng**
"The cafeteria is good."	"good cafeteria"
Shìr xiǎo.	**xiǎo shìr**
"The matter is small."	"small matter"
Yàngzi lǎo.	**lǎo yàngzi**
"The appearance is old."	"old appearance, old way"

2. Transform the following verbs to the negative with **bù**. Remember that before syllables in Tone Four, **bù** changes from Tone Four to Tone Two to become **bú**.

máng	**bù máng**
"busy"	"not busy"
jǐnzhāng	**bù jǐnzhāng**
"nervous"	"not nervous"
lèi	**bú lèi**
"tired"	"not tired"
xiǎo	**bù xiǎo**
"little"	"not little"
lǎo	**bù lǎo**
"old"	"not old"
kùn	**bú kùn**
"sleepy"	"not sleepy"
nán	**bù nán**
"hard"	"not hard"
róngyi	**bù róngyi**
"easy"	"not easy"
qù	**bú qù**
"go"	"not go"

3. Change the following sentences into the negative by adding **bù** or **bú**.

Wǒ huí sùshè.

"I'm going back to the dormitory."

Wǒ bù huí sùshè.

"I'm not going back to the dormitory."

Tāmen hǎo ma?

"Are they well?"

Tāmen bù hǎo ma?

"Are they not well?"

Nǐ háizi lèi ma?

"Is your child tired?"

Nǐ háizi bú lèi ma?

"Is your child not tired?"

Nǐmen hěn máng.

"You are very busy."

Nǐmen bù hěn máng.

"You are not very busy."

Bàba qù gōngzuò.

"Father goes to work."

Bàba bú qù gōngzuò.

"Father does not go to work."

Xuéxí Zhōngwén nán ma?

"Is learning Chinese hard?"

Xuéxí Zhōngwén bù nán ma?

"Is learning Chinese not hard?"

4. Change the following statements into questions by using the positive-negative question pattern.

Tā qù.

"She is going."

Tā qù bu qù?

"Is she going or not?"

Nǐ hěn kùn.

"You are sleepy."

Nǐ kùn bu kùn?

"Are you sleepy or not?"

Tāmen hěn máng.

"They are busy."

Tāmen máng bu máng?

"Are they busy or not?"

Bàba hěn lèi.

"Dad is tired."

Bàba lèi bu lèi?

"Is Dad tired or not?"

Māma hěn gāo.

"Mom is tall."

Māma gāo bu gāo?

"Is Mom tall or not?"

Tā hěn hǎo.

"He is good."

Tā hǎo bu hǎo?

"Is he good or not?"

Zhōngwén hěn nán.

"Chinese is hard."

Zhōngwén nán bu nán?

"Is Chinese hard or not?"

5. Convert the following **ma** questions into positive-negative questions.

Nǐ zuìjìn hǎo ma?

"Have you been well recently?"

Nǐ zuìjìn hǎo bu hǎo?

"Have you been well recently or not?"

Tā qù túshūguǎn ma?

"Does he go to the library?"

Tā qù bu qù túshūguǎn?

"Does he go to the library or not?"

Zhōngwén róngyi ma?

"Is Chinese easy?"

Zhōngwén róngyi bu róngyi?

"Is Chinese easy or not?"

Nǐ gōngzuò jǐnzhāng ma?

"Is your work intense?"

Nǐ gōngzuò jǐnzhāng bu jǐnzhāng?

"Is your work intense or not?"

Tā àirén ǎi ma?

"Is her spouse short?"

Tā àirén ǎi bu ǎi?

"Is her spouse short or not?"

Nǐmen qù shítáng ma?

"Do you go to the cafeteria?"

Nǐmen qù bu qù shítáng?

"Do you go to the cafeteria or not?"

6. First listen to each comment about **Xiǎo Wáng**, then make a comment about yourself using **bú tài**.

Xiǎo Wáng hěn kùn.

"Little Wang is very sleepy."

Wǒ bú tài kùn.

"I am not too sleepy."

Xiǎo Wáng hěn lèi.

"Little Wang is very tired."

Wǒ bú tài lèi.

"I am not too tired."

Xiǎo Wáng hěn gāo.

"Little Wang is very tall."

Wǒ bú tài gāo.

"I am not too tall."

Xiǎo Wáng zuìjìn hěn hǎo.

"Little Wang has been very well recently."

Wǒ zuìjìn bú tài hǎo.

"I have not been too well recently."

Xiǎo Wáng hěn lǎo.

"Little Wang is very old."

Wǒ bú tài lǎo.

"I am not too old."

Xiǎo Wáng gōngzuò hěn jǐnzhāng.

"Little Wang is very nervous at work."

Wǒ gōngzuò bú tài jǐnzhāng.

"I am not too nervous at work."

7. Transform the following sentences from the **hěn** + STATIVE VERB pattern to the **tǐng...-de** pattern.

Tā hěn kùn.

"He is very sleepy."

Tā tǐng kùnde.

"He is quite sleepy."

Zhōngwén hěn nán.

"Chinese is very hard."

Zhōngwén tǐng nánde.

"Chinese is quite hard."

Wǒ māma hěn máng.

"My mother is very busy."

Wǒ māma tǐng mángde.

"My mother is quite busy."

Nǐ àirén hěn ǎi.

"Your spouse is very short."

Nǐ àirén tǐng ǎide.

"Your spouse is quite short."

Tā bàba hěn lǎo.

"Her father is very old."

Tā bàba tǐng lǎode.

"Her father is quite old."

Nǐ yàngzi hěn jǐnzhāng.

"You look like you're very nervous."

Nǐ yàngzi tǐng jǐnzhāngde.

"You look like you're quite nervous."

Tā zuìjìn gōngzuò hěn lèi.

"He is very tired from work lately."

Tā zuìjìn gōngzuò tǐng lèide.

"He is quite tired from work lately."

Unit 1, Part 4: Transformation and Response Drills

1. Add the surname and title of the wife to the husband's surname and title.

   Zhào Xiānsheng   **Zhào Xiānsheng, Zhào Tàitai.**
   "Mr. Zhao"   "Mr. and Mrs. Zhao"

   Gāo Xiānsheng   **Gāo Xiānsheng, Gāo Tàitai.**
   "Mr. Gao"   "Mr. and Mrs. Gao"

   Wáng Xiānsheng   **Wáng Xiānsheng, Wáng Tàitai**
   "Mr. Wang"   "Mr. and Mrs. Wang"

   Kē Xiānsheng   **Kē Xiānsheng, Kē Tàitai**
   "Mr. Ke"   "Mr. and Mrs. Ke"

   Lín Xiānsheng   **Lín Xiānsheng, Lín Tàitai**
   "Mr. Lin"   "Mr. and Mrs. Lin"

   Xiè Xiānsheng   **Xiè Xiānsheng, Xiè Tàitai**
   "Mr. Xie"   "Mr. and Mrs. Xie"

2. Add the title **Xiáojie** to each of the following surnames.

   Wáng   **Wáng Xiáojie**
   "Wang"   "Miss/Ms. Wang"

   Lín   **Lín Xiáojie**
   "Lin"   "Miss/Ms. Lin"

   Hé   **Hé Xiáojie**
   "He"   "Miss/Ms. He"

   Xiè   **Xiè Xiáojie**
   "Xie"   "Miss/Ms. Xie"

   Gāo   **Gāo Xiáojie**
   "Gao"   "Miss/Ms. Gao"

   Zhào   **Zhào Xiáojie**
   "Zhao"   "Miss/Ms. Zhao"

3. Add the title **Lǎoshī** to each of the following surnames.

   Lín   **Lín Lǎoshī**
   "Lin"   "Teacher Lin"

   Xiè   **Xiè Lǎoshī**
   "Xie"   "Teacher Xie"

   Gāo   **Gāo Lǎoshī**
   "Gao"   "Teacher Gao"

Zhào	**Zhào Lǎoshī**
"Zhao"	"Teacher Zhao"
Hé	**Hé Lǎoshī**
"He"	"Teacher He"
Wáng	**Wáng Lǎoshī**
"Wang"	"Teacher Wang"

4. Add **qǐng** to the following sentences to create polite imperatives.

Nǐ qù shítáng.	**Qǐng nǐ qù shítáng.**
"You go to the cafeteria."	"Please go to the cafeteria."
Nǐ qù gōngzuò.	**Qǐng nǐ qù gōngzuò.**
"You go work."	"Please go work."
Tā huí sùshè.	**Qǐng tā huí sùshè.**
"He goes back to the dormitory."	"Ask him to please go back to the dormitory."
Nǐmen qù túshūguǎn bàn yìdiǎnr shì.	**Qǐng nǐmen qù túshūguǎn bàn yìdiǎnr shì.**
"You go to the library and take care of some stuff."	"Please go to the library and take care of some stuff."
Tāmen xiān zǒu.	**Qǐng tāmen xiān zǒu.**
"They leave earlier."	"Ask them to please leave earlier."

5. Add changed status **le** to the following sentences.

Wǒ děi qù gōngzuò.	**Wǒ děi qù gōngzuòle.**
"I have to go to work."	"I have to go to work now."
Tā zěmmeyàng?	**Tā zěmmeyàng le?**
"How is he?"	"What happened to him?"
Tā xiān zǒu.	**Tā xiān zǒule.**
"She leaves earlier."	"She left earlier already."
Xiǎo Lín qù shítáng.	**Xiǎo Lín qù shítáng le.**
"Little Lin goes to the cafeteria."	"Little Lin went to the cafeteria."
Shéi bú qù?	**Shéi bú qùle?**
"Who is not going?"	"Who is not going now?"
Tāmen huí sùshè.	**Tāmen huí sùshè le.**
"They go back to the dormitory."	"They went back to the dormitory."

6. Add changed status **le** to the following questions ending in **ma**.

Tā māma hǎo ma?	**Tā māma hǎole ma?**
"Is her mother well?"	"Has her mother gotten well?"
Nǐ jǐnzhāng ma?	**Nǐ jǐnzhāngle ma?**
"Are you nervous?"	"Have you gotten nervous?"

Wǒmen kéyi huí sùshè ma?

"Can we go back to the dormitory?"

Tā qù túshūguǎn bàn shì ma?

"Is he going to the library to take care of some stuff?"

Háizi kùn ma?

"Are the kids sleepy?"

Nǐmen qù shítáng ma?

"Are you going to the cafeteria?"

Wǒmen kéyi huí sùshè le ma?

"Can we go back to the dormitory now?"

Tā qù túshūguǎn bàn shì le ma?

"Has he gone to the library to take care of some stuff?"

Háizi kùnle ma?

"Have the kids gotten sleepy?"

Nǐmen qù shítáng le ma?

"Have you gone to the cafeteria?"

Unit 2, Part 1: Transformation and Response Drills

1. Respond to the following questions with an equative verb sentence beginning with **shì**.

Tā shi Měiguo rén ma?   **Shì, tā shi Měiguo rén.**

"Is she American?"   "Yes, she is American."

Tā shi Zhōngguo rén ma?   **Shì, tā shi Zhōngguo rén.**

"Is he Chinese?"   "Yes, he is Chinese."

Tā shi Wáng Lǎoshī ma?   **Shì, tā shi Wáng Lǎoshī.**

"Is she Teacher Wang?"   "Yes, she is Teacher Wang."

Tā shi nǐ àirén ma?   **Shì, tā shi wǒ àirén.**

"Is he your spouse?"   "Yes, he is my spouse."

Nǐ shi tā bàba ma?   **Shì, wǒ shi tā bàba.**

"Are you her father?"   "Yes, I am her father."

Nǐ shi tā māma ma?   **Shì, wǒ shi tā māma.**

"Are you his mother?"   "Yes, I am his mother."

2. Respond to the following questions with a negative equative verb sentence beginning with **bú shi**.

Nǐ shi Zhōngwén lǎoshī ma?   **Bú shi, wǒ bú shi Zhōngwén lǎoshī.**

"Are you a Chinese teacher?"   "No, I am not a Chinese teacher."

Nǐ shi Lín Xiáojie ma?   **Bú shi, wǒ bú shi Lín Xiáojie.**

"Are you Ms. Lin?"   "No, I am not Ms. Lin."

Nǐmen shi Jiā'nádà rén ma?   **Bú shi, wǒmen bú shi Jiā'nádà rén.**

"Are you all Canadian?"   "No, we're not Canadian."

Tā shi Wáng Xiānsheng ma?   **Bú shi, tā bú shi Wáng Xiānsheng.**

"Is he Mr. Wang?"   "No, he's not Mr. Wang."

3. Respond to the following questions either with an equative verb sentence beginning with **Shì** or with a negative equative verb sentence beginning with **Bú shi**, depending on the cue provided.

Tā shi nǐ bàba ma? (Shì.)   **Shì, tā shi wǒ bàba.**

"Is he your dad?" ("Yes.")   "Yes, he is my dad."

Tā shi nǐ māma ma? (Bú shi.)   **Bú shi, tā bú shi wǒ māma.**

"Is she your mom?" ("No.")   "No, she's not my mom."

Qǐng wèn, nǐ shi Bái Lǎoshī ma? (Bú shi.)   **Bú shi, wǒ bú shi Bái Lǎoshī.**

"Excuse me, are you Teacher Bai?" ("No.")   "No, I'm not Teacher Bai."

Tā shi Huáyì Měiguo rén ma? (Shì.)   **Shì, tā shi Huáyì Měiguo rén.**

"Is he an American of Chinese descent?" ("Yes.")   "Yes, he's an American of Chinese descent."

Nǐmen shi Táiwān rén ma? (Bú shi.)   **Bú shi, wǒmen bú shi Táiwān rén.**

"Are you Taiwanese?" ("No.")   "No, we're not Taiwanese."

4. Transform the following statements into questions using **shì bu shi**.

Tā shi Rìběn rén.

"He is Japanese."

Tā shì bu shi Rìběn rén?

"Is he Japanese?"

Nǐ shi tā àirén.

"You are her spouse."

Nǐ shì bu shi tā àirén?

"Are you her spouse?"

Nǐmen shi Xībānyá rén.

"You are Spanish."

Nǐmen shì bu shi Xībānyá rén?

"Are you Spanish?"

Tā shi Wáng Xiáojie.

"She is Miss Wang."

Tā shì bu shi Wáng Xiáojie?

"Is she Miss Wang?"

Nǐ zuìjìn hěn máng.

"You have been very busy recently."

Nǐ zuìjìn shì bu shi hěn máng?

"Have you been very busy lately?"

Tā dào túshūguǎn qù.

"He is going to the library."

Tā shì bu shi dào túshūguǎn qù?

"Is it the case that he's going to the library?"

5. Answer the following questions about nationality using the cues provided.

Tā shi něiguó rén? (Jiā'nádà rén)

"What nationality is he?" ("Canadian")

Tā shi Jiā'nádà rén.

"He's Canadian."

Nǐ àirén shi něiguó rén? (Rìběn rén)

"What nationality is your spouse?" ("Japanese")

Tā shi Rìběn rén.

"She's Japanese."

Nín shi něiguó rén? (Měiguo rén)

"What nationality are you?" ("American")

Wǒ shi Měiguo rén.

"I'm American."

Mǎ Xiáojie shi něiguó rén? (Zhōngguo rén)

"What nationality is Ms. Ma?"

Mǎ Xiáojie shi Zhōngguo rén.

"Ms. Ma is Chinese."

Xiǎo Lín shi něiguó rén? (Mǎláixīyà rén)

"What nationality is Little Lin?" ("Malaysian")

Xiǎo Lín shi Mǎláixīyà rén.

"Little Lin is Malaysian."

Nǐ lǎoshī shi něiguó rén? (Xīnjiāpō rén)

"What nationality is your teacher?" ("Singaporean")

Wǒ lǎoshī shi Xīnjiāpō rén.

"My teacher is Singaporean."

6. Respond to the following questions about someone's name using the cues provided.

Tā jiào shémme míngzi? (Hé Zhìwén)

"What is his name?"

Tā jiào Hé Zhìwén.

"He is called He Zhiwen."

Nǐ àirén jiào shémme míngzi? (Wáng Dàmíng)

"What is your spouse's name?"

Wǒ àirén jiào Wáng Dàmíng.

"My spouse is called Wang Daming."

Nǐ māma jiào shémme míngzi? (Xiè Wéntíng)

"What is your mom's name?"

Wǒ māma jiào Xiè Wéntíng.

"My mom's name is Xie Wenting."

Nǐ bàba jiào shémme míngzi? (Zhào Guólì)

"What is your dad's name?"

Wǒ bàba jiào Zhào Guólì.

"My dad's name is Zhao Guoli."

Nǐ jiào shémme míngzi? (give your own name)

"What is your name?"

Wǒ jiào...

"My name is..."

7. Negate the following sentences by placing a **bù** before the **dōu**.

Tāmen dōu shi Zhōngguo rén.

"They are all Chinese."

Tāmen bù dōu shi Zhōngguo rén.

"They are not all Chinese."

Tāmen dōu hěn kùn.

"They are all very sleepy."

Tāmen bù dōu hěn kùn.

"They are not all very sleepy."

Wǒmen dōu huí sùshè.

"We are all going back to the dorm."

Wǒmen bù dōu huí sùshè.

"We are not all going back to the dorm."

Wǒmen dōu shi Huáyì Měiguo rén.

"We are all Chinese-Americans."

Wǒmen bù dōu shi Huáyì Měiguo rén.

"We are not all Chinese-Americans."

Nǐmen dōu shi hǎo háizi!

"You are all good children!"

Nǐmen bù dōu shi hǎo háizi!

"You are not all good children!"

Dōu shi xiǎo shì.

"They are all small matters."

Bù dōu shi xiǎo shì.

"They are not all small matters."

8. Disagree with your interlocutor. Answer "It's not THIS person, it's THAT person!" etc.

Shì zhèige rén ma?

"Is it this person?"

Bú shi zhèige rén, shi nèige rén!

"It's not this person, it's that person!"

Shì zhèige háizi ma?

"Was it this kid?"

Bú shi zhèige háizi, shi nèige háizi!

"It wasn't this kid, it was that kid!"

Shì zhèiwèi lǎoshī ma?

"Is it this teacher?"

Bú shi zhèiwèi lǎoshī, shi nèiwèi lǎoshī!

"It isn't this teacher, it's that teacher!"

Shì zhèiwèi tóngxué ma?

"Is it this classmate?"

Bú shi zhèiwèi tóngxué, shi nèiwèi tóngxué!

"It isn't this classmate, it's that classmate!"

Shì zhèige míngzi ma?

"Was it this name?"

Bú shi zhèige míngzi, shi nèige míngzi!

"It wasn't this name, it was that name!"

Shì zhèige sùshè ma?

"Was it this dormitory?"

Bú shi zhèige sùshè, shi nèige sùshè!

"It wasn't this dormitory, it was that dormitory!"

9. Respond to the questions with **něi-** "which?" by using **nèi-** "that."

Shì něige rén?

"Which person was it?"

Shì nèige rén!

"It was that person!"

Shì něige háizi?

"Which child was it?"

Shì nèige háizi!

"It was that child!"

Shì něiwèi lǎoshī?

"Which teacher is it?"

Shì nèiwèi lǎoshī!

"It's that teacher!"

Shì něiwèi tóngxué?

"Which classmate is it?"

Shì nèiwèi tóngxué!

"It's that classmate!"

Shì něige gōngzuò?	**Shì nèige gōngzuò!**
"Which job was it?"	"It was that job!"
Shì něige shítáng?	**Shì nèige shítáng!**
"Which dining hall was it?"	"It was that dining hall!"

10. Confirm the truth of what your interlocutor says about the first person by repeating it, but add the new and different information about the other person that is given in the cue by using **kěshi**.

Lǎo Wáng shi Měiguo rén. (Xiǎo Lín, Mǎláixīyà rén)

"Old Wang is American." ("Little Lin, Malaysian")

Lǎo Wáng shi Měiguo rén, kěshi Xiǎo Lín shi Mǎláixīyà rén.

"Old Wang is American, but Little Lin is Malaysian."

Lǎo Bái shi Měiguo rén. (Xiǎo Hé, Xībānyá rén)

"Old Bai is American." ("Little He, Spanish")

Lǎo Bái shi Měiguo rén, kěshi Xiǎo Hé shi Xībānyá rén.

"Old Bai is American, but Little He is Spanish."

Lǎo Gāo shi Zhōngguo rén. (Xiǎo Zhào, Rìběn rén)

"Old Gao is Chinese." ("Little Zhao, Japanese")

Lǎo Gāo shi Zhōngguo rén, kěshi Xiǎo Zhào shi Rìběn rén.

"Old Gao is Chinese, but Little Zhao is Japanese."

Lǎo Lǐ shi Táiwān rén. (Xiǎo Kē, Xīnjiāpō rén)

"Old Li is Taiwanese." ("Little Ke, Singaporean")

Lǎo Lǐ shi Táiwān rén, kěshi Xiǎo Kē shi Xīnjiāpō rén.

"Old Li is Taiwanese, but Little Ke is Singaporean."

. . . .

Unit 2, Part 2: Transformation and Response Drills

1. Combine the first noun or pronoun with the noun that follows by adding -de.

wǒ, àirén

"I, spouse"

wǒde àirén

"my spouse"

Lǎo Chén, tóngxué

"Old Chen, classmate"

Lǎo Chénde tóngxué

"Old Chen's classmate"

tā, bàba

"he/she, father"

tāde bàba

"his/her father"

nǐmen, sùshè

"you all, dormitory"

nǐmende sùshè

"your dormitory"

tāmen, māma

"they, mother"

tāmende māma

"their mother"

Zhào tóngxué, tóngwū

"classmate Zhao, roommate"

Zhào tóngxuéde tóngwū

"classmate Zhao's roommate"

2. Transform the sentences with **lái** or **qù** followed directly by a place word to the **dào...lái** or **dào...qù** pattern.

Hěn gāoxìng nǐ lái Běijīng!

"I'm glad you've come to Beijing!"

Hěn gāoxìng nǐ dào Běijīng lái!

"I'm glad you've come to Beijing!"

Huānyíng nǐ lái Táiwān!

"Welcome to Taiwan!"

Huānyíng nǐ dào Táiwān lái!

"Welcome to Taiwan!"

Qǐng nǐ qù wǒde sùshè.

"Please go to my dormitory."

Qǐng nǐ dào wǒde sùshè qù.

"Please go to my dormitory."

Búyào qù túshūguǎn!

"Don't go to the library!"

Búyào dào túshūguǎn qù!

"Don't go to the library!"

Tā qù Rìběn le.

"He went to Japan."

Tā dào Rìběn qùle.

"He has gone to Japan."

Nǐ yīnggāi lái wǒde gōngsī.

"You should come to my company."

Nǐ yīnggāi dào wǒde gōngsī lái.

"You should come to my company."

3. Change the following imperative sentences to negative imperatives by using **bié**.

Qǐng nǐ qù gōngzuò.

"Please go to work."

Qǐng nǐ bié qù gōngzuò.

"Please don't go to work."

Qǐng tāmen lái Táiwān.

"Ask them to come to Taiwan."

Qǐng tāmen bié lái Táiwān.

"Ask them not to come to Taiwan."

Chén Xiáojie, qǐng zuò.

"Miss Chen, please sit."

Chén Xiáojie, qǐng bié zuò.

"Miss Chen, please don't sit."

Bàba, qǐng zǒu.

"Father, please go."

Bàba, qǐng bié zǒu.

"Father, please don't go."

Qǐng nǐmen jiào wǒ Lǎo Chén.

"You all please call me Old Chen."

Qǐng nǐmen bié jiào wǒ Lǎo Chén.

"You all please don't call me Old Chen."

4. Change the following negative imperative sentences with **búyào** to positive imperatives by deleting the **búyào**.

Qǐng nǐ búyào qù túshūguǎn.

"Please don't go to the library."

Qǐng nǐ qù túshūguǎn.

"Please go to the library."

Qǐng nǐ búyào huí sùshè.

"Please don't go back to the dormitory."

Qǐng nǐ huí sùshè.

"Please go back to the dormitory."

Qǐng tāmen búyào lái Měiguo.

"Ask them not to come to the States."

Qǐng tāmen lái Měiguo.

"Ask them to come to the States."

Qǐng nǐmen búyào qù Zhōngguo.

"Please don't go to China."

Qǐng nǐmen qù Zhōngguo.

"Please go to China."

Qǐng nǐ búyào zèmme chēnghu wǒ.

"Please don't address me in this way."

Qǐng nǐ zèmme chēnghu wǒ.

"Please address me in this way."

Qǐng nǐmen búyào qù gōngzuò.

"Please don't go to work."

Qǐng nǐmen qù gōngzuò.

"Please go to work."

5. Respond to each question using the cue provided.

Zhè shi shéide lǎoshī? (wǒde)

"This is whose teacher?" ("my")

Zhè shi wǒde lǎoshī.

"This is my teacher."

Zhè shi shéide háizi? (nǐde)

"Whose kid is this?" ("your")

Zhè shi nǐde háizi.

"This is your kid."

Zhè shi shéide bàba? (tāmende)

"Whose father is this?" ("their")

Zhè shi tāmende bàba.

"This is their father."

Nà shi shéide àirén? (wǒde)

"Whose spouse is that?" ("my")

Nà shi wǒde àirén.

"That is my spouse."

Nà shi shéide māma? (tāmende)

"Whose mother is that?" ("their")

Nà shi tāmende māma.

"That is their mother."

Zhè shi shéide tóngxué? (nǐmende)

"Whose classmate is this?" ("your")

Zhè shi nǐmende tóngxué.

"This is your classmate."

Unit 2, Part 3: Transformation and Response Drills

1. Transform the polite questions with **guìxìng** to more ordinary questions with **xìng shémme**. Remember also to change polite **nín** to ordinary **nǐ**.

Nín guìxìng?

"What's your last name?"

Nèiwèi nǚshì guìxìng?

"What's that lady's last name?"

Nèiwèi lǎoshī guìxìng?

"What's that teacher's last name?"

Qǐng wèn, xiáojie, nín guìxìng?

"Excuse me, Miss, what's your last name?"

Zhèiwèi dàxué xiàozhǎng guìxìng?

"What's this college president's last name?"

Nǐ xìng shémme?

"What's your last name?"

Nèiwèi nǚshì xìng shémme?

"What's that lady's last name?"

Nèiwèi lǎoshī xìng shémme?

"What's that teacher's last name?"

Qǐng wèn, xiáojie, nǐ xìng shémme?

"Excuse me, Miss, what's your last name?"

Zhèiwèi dàxué xiàozhǎng xìng shémme?

"What's this college president's last name?"

2. Explain that, by golly, your roommate, classmate, colleague, etc. has the same surname as the speaker's!

Wǒde tóngwū xìng Gāo.

"My roommate's last name is Gao."

Wǒde tóngxué xìng Lín.

"My classmate's last name is Lin."

Wǒde tóngshì xìng Chén.

"My colleague's last name is Chen."

Wǒde Zhōngwén lǎoshī xìng Wú.

"My Chinese teacher's last name is Wu."

Wǒ māma xìng Mǎ.

"My mom's last name is Ma."

Wǒmende xiàozhǎng xìng Hé.

"Our college president's surname is He."

Wǒde tóngwū yě xìng Gāo!

"My roommate's last name is also Gao!"

Wǒde tóngxué yě xìng Lín!

"My classmate's last name is also Lin!"

Wǒde tóngshì yě xìng Chén!

"My colleague's last name is also Chen!"

Wǒde Zhōngwén lǎoshī yě xìng Wú!

"My Chinese teacher's last name is also Wu!"

Wǒ māma yě xìng Mǎ!

"My mom's last name is also Ma!"

Wǒmende xiàozhǎng yě xìng Hé!

"Our college president's surname is also He!"

3. Add **ba** to the following sentences to indicate that you think what you said is probably so.

Nǐ yě shi lǎoshī.

"You are a teacher, too."

Tā shi nǐde tóngshì.

"She is your co-worker."

Xiǎo Zhào bú shi Zhōngguo rén.

"Little Zhao is not Chinese."

Nǐ zài Wàijiāobù gōngzuò.

"You work at the Foreign Ministry."

Nǐ yě shi lǎoshī ba?

"You are a teacher too, I guess?"

Tā shi nǐde tóngshì ba?

"She is your co-worker, I suppose?"

Xiǎo Zhào bú shi Zhōngguo rén ba?

"I suppose Little Zhao is not Chinese?"

Nǐ zài Wàijiāobù gōngzuò ba?

"I guess you work at the Foreign Ministry?"

Chén Xiáojie shi Mǎláixīyà rén.

"Miss Chen is Malaysian."

Chén Xiáojie shi Mǎláixīyà rén ba?

"Miss Chen is Malaysian, I guess?"

Tāmen bú rènshi nǐ.

"They are not acquainted with you."

Tāmen bú rènshi nǐ ba?

"They are not acquainted with you, I assume?"

4. Respond to the following questions using the cue provided.

Nǐ zài nǎr gōngzuò a? (shítáng)

"Where do you work?" ("cafeteria")

Wǒ zài shítáng gōngzuò.

"I work at the cafeteria."

Nǐmen zài nǎr gōngzuò a? (dàshǐguǎn)

"Where do you all work?" ("embassy")

Wǒmen zài dàshǐguǎn gōngzuò.

"We work at the embassy."

Tā zài nǎr gōngzuò a? (dàxué)

"Where does she work?" ("university")

Tā zài dàxué gōngzuò.

"She works at the university."

Tāmen zài nǎr gōngzuò a? (túshūguǎn)

"Where do they work?" ("library")

Tāmen zài túshūguǎn gōngzuò.

"They work at the library."

Xiǎo Chén zài nǎr gōngzuò a? (gōngsī)

"Where does Little Chen work?" ("company")

Xiǎo Chén zài gōngsī gōngzuò.

"Little Chen works at the company."

Lǎo Zhào zài nǎr gōngzuò a? (Wàijiāobù)

"Where does Old Zhao work?" ("Foreign Ministry")

Lǎo Zhào zài Wàijiāobù gōngzuò.

"Old Zhao works at the Foreign Ministry."

Unit 2, Part 4: Transformation and Response Drills

1. Transform the following sentences from **bù** to past negative with **méi**.

   Wǒ bù lái.
   "I'm not coming."

   Wǒ méi lái.
   "I didn't come."

   Wǒ bù zǒu.
   "I'm not leaving."

   Wǒ méi zǒu.
   "I didn't leave."

   Wǒ bú dài míngpiàn.
   "I don't carry name cards."

   Wǒ méi dài míngpiàn.
   "I didn't carry name cards."

   Tā bú qù Zhōngguo.
   "She's not going to China."

   Tā méi qù Zhōngguo.
   "She didn't go to China."

   Nǐ yě bú wèn zěmme qù.
   "And you don't ask how to go."

   Nǐ yě méi wèn zěmme qù.
   "And you didn't ask how to go."

   Nǐmen bù huí sùshè ma?
   "You're not going back to the dorm?"

   Nǐmen méi huí sùshè ma?
   "You didn't go back to the dorm?"

   Nǐmen bú qù gōngsī ma?
   "You're not going to the company?"

   Nǐmen méi qù gōngsī ma?
   "You didn't go to the company?"

2. Transform the following sentences with the coverb **zài** describing where someone works to noun phrases with **-de** that indicate a person's affiliation.

   Nèiwèi Shī Xiáojie zài Zhōng-Měi Màoyì Gōngsī gōngzuò.
   "That Miss Shi works at the Sino-American Trading Company."

   Zhōng-Měi Màoyì Gōngsīde nèiwèi Shī Xiáojie
   "that Miss Shi from Sino-American trading company"

   Nèiwèi Mǎ Xiáojie zài Měiguo Dàshǐguǎn gōngzuò.
   "That Ms. Ma works at the American Embassy."

   Měiguo Dàshǐguǎnde nèiwèi Mǎ Xiáojie
   "that Ms. Ma from the American Embassy"

   Nèiwèi Hé Lǎoshī zài Táiwān Dàxué gōngzuò.
   "That Prof. He works at Taiwan University."

   Táiwān Dàxuéde nèiwèi Hé Lǎoshī
   "that Prof. He from Taiwan University"

   Nèiwèi Wú Xiáojie zài Wàijiāobù gōngzuò.
   "That Miss Wu works at the Foreign Ministry."

   Wàijiāobùde nèiwèi Wú Xiáojie
   "that Miss Wu from the Foreign Ministry"

3. Transform the sentences with **bù dōu** to **dōu bù**.

   Tāmen bù dōu shi Rìběn rén.
   "They are not all Japanese."

   Tāmen dōu bú shi Rìběn rén.
   "They all are not Japanese."

   Wǒmen bù dōu zài Wàijiāobù gōngzuò.
   "We don't all work at the Foreign Ministry."

   Wǒmen dōu bú zài Wàijiāobù gōngzuò.
   "We all don't work at the Foreign Ministry."

   Tāmen bù dōu rènshi Wáng Xiáojie.
   "They don't all know Ms. Wang."

   Tāmen dōu bú rènshi Wáng Xiáojie.
   "None of them knows Ms. Wang."

Wǒmen bù dōu xuéxí Zhōngwén.

"We don't all learn Chinese."

Tāmen bù dōu huānyíng wǒ dào Běijīng qù.

"Not all of them welcome me to go to Beijing."

Wǒmen dōu bù xuéxí Zhōngwén.

"None of us is learning Chinese."

Tāmen dōu bù huānyíng wǒ dào Běijīng qù.

"None of them welcomes me to go to Beijing."

4. Transform the expressions with **zhèi-** to **nèi-** and also add **yě**.

Zhèiwèi xiānsheng xìng Wáng.

"This gentleman's last name is Wang."

Nèiwèi xiānsheng yě xìng Wáng.

"That gentleman's last name is also Wang."

Zhèiwèi tàitai xìng Bái.

"This lady's last name is Bai."

Nèiwèi tàitai yě xìng Bái.

"That lady's last name is also Bai."

Zhèiwèi xiáojie xìng Lín.

"This young lady's last name is Lin."

Nèiwèi xiáojie yě xìng Lín.

"That young lady's last name is also Lin."

Zhèige háizi hěn lèi.

"This child is very tired."

Nèige háizi yě hěn lèi.

"That child is also very tired."

Zhèiwèi jīnglǐ hěn gāoxìng.

"This manager is very happy."

Nèiwèi jīnglǐ yě hěn gāoxìng.

"That manager is also very happy."

Zhèige Měiguo rén wǒ bú rènshì.

"I don't know this American."

Nèige Měiguo rén wǒ yě bú rènshì.

"I don't know that American either."

Zhèige dàxué hěn xīn.

"This university is very new."

Nèige dàxué yě hěn xīn.

"That university is also very new."

5. Use **gēn** to join the second noun or pronoun to the first noun or pronoun.

wǒ (nǐ)

"I" ("you")

wǒ gēn nǐ

"I and you"

wǒ (tā)

"I" ("he")

wǒ gēn tā

"I and he"

wǒmen (nǐmen)

"we" ("you")

wǒmen gēn nǐmen

"we and you"

wǒmen (tāmen)

"we" ("they")

wǒmen gēn tāmen

"we and they"

Lǎo Lǐ (Xiǎo Bái)

"Old Li" ("Little Bai")

Lǎo Lǐ gēn Xiǎo Bái

"Old Li and Little Bai"

àirén (háizi)

"spouse" ("child")

àirén gēn háizi

"spouse and child"

xiānsheng (tàitai)

"husband" ("wife")

xiānsheng gēn tàitai

"husband and wife"

Zhōngguo (Táiwān)

"Mainland China" ("Taiwan")

Zhōngguo gēn Táiwān

"Mainland China and Taiwan"

Zhōngguo rén (Měiguo rén)

"Chinese" ("Americans")

Zhōngguo rén gēn Měiguo rén

"Chinese and Americans"

6. Transform each phrase or sentence that you hear into a politer equivalent.

Nǐ hǎo!

"How are you?"

Nín hǎo!

"How do you do?"

Nǐ xìng shémme?

"What's your last name?"

Nín guìxìng?

"What is your honorable surname?"

zhèige xiānsheng

"this man"

zhèiwèi xiānsheng

"this gentleman"

nèige tàitai

"that lady"

nèiwèi tàitai

"that lady"

Něige xiáojie?

"Which young woman?"

Něiwèi xiáojie?

"Which young lady?"

zhèige xiàozhǎng

"this school principal"

zhèiwèi xiàozhǎng

"this school principal"

nèige zǒngjīnglǐ

"that general manager"

nèiwèi zǒngjīnglǐ

"that general manager"

Něige nǚshì?

"Which lady?"

Něiwèi nǚshì?

"Which lady?"

yíge lǎoshī

"a teacher"

yíwèi lǎoshī

"a teacher"

Unit 3, Part 1: Transformation and Response Drills

1. Say the number that comes after the number you hear.

liù
"six"

qī
"seven"

jiǔ
"nine"

shí
"ten"

yī
"one"

èr
"two"

sì
"four"

wǔ
"five"

qī
"seven"

bā
"eight"

èr
"two"

sān
"three"

bā
"eight"

jiǔ
"nine"

sān
"three"

sì
"four"

wǔ
"five"

liù
"six"

2. Say the number that comes before the number you hear.

qī
"seven"

liù
"six"

shí
"ten"

jiǔ
"nine"

èr
"two"

yī
"one"

jiǔ
"nine"

bā
"eight"

wǔ
"five"

sì
"four"

sān
"three"

èr
"two"

liù
"six"

wǔ
"five"

bā	**qī**
"eight"	"seven"
sì	**sān**
"four"	"three"

3. Comment that, in each case, you have one more student in your class than the speaker does.

Wǒmen bānshang yǒu jiǔge tóngxué.

"Our class has nine classmates."

Wǒmen bānshang yǒu liǎngge tóngxué.

"Our class has two classmates."

Wǒmen bānshang yǒu liùge tóngxué.

"Our class has six classmates."

Wǒmen bānshang yǒu sìge tóngxué.

"Our class has four classmates."

Wǒmen bānshang yǒu sān'ge tóngxué.

"Our class has three classmates."

Wǒmen bānshang yǒu qīge tóngxué.

"Our class has seven classmates."

Wǒmen bānshang yǒu wǔge tóngxué.

"Our class has five classmates."

Wǒmen bānshang yǒu bāge tóngxué.

"Our class has eight classmates."

Wǒmen bānshang yǒu shíge tóngxué.

"Our class has ten classmates."

Wǒmen bānshang yǒu sān'ge tóngxué.

"Our class has three classmates."

Wǒmen bānshang yǒu qīge tóngxué.

"Our class has seven classmates."

Wǒmen bānshang yǒu wǔge tóngxué.

"Our class has five classmates."

Wǒmen bānshang yǒu sìge tóngxué.

"Our class has four classmates."

Wǒmen bānshang yǒu bāge tóngxué.

"Our class has eight classmates."

Wǒmen bānshang yǒu liùge tóngxué.

"Our class has six classmates."

Wǒmen bānshang yǒu jiǔge tóngxué.

"Our class has nine classmates."

4. Comment that, in each case, the ratio of male students to female students in your class is the exact reverse of the speaker's class.

Wǒmen bānshang yǒu liǎngge nánshēng, yíge nǚshēng.

"Our class has two guys, one girl."

Wǒmen bānshang yǒu sān'ge nánshēng, sìge nǚshēng.

"Our class has three guys, four girls."

Wǒmen bānshang yǒu wǔge nánshēng, liùge nǚshēng.

"Our class has five guys, six girls."

Wǒmen bānshang yǒu qīge nánshēng, bāge nǚshēng.

"Our class has seven guys, eight girls."

Wǒmen bānshang yǒu jiǔge nánshēng, shíge nǚshēng.

"Our class has nine guys, ten girls."

Wǒmen bānshang yǒu yíge nánshēng, liǎngge nǚshēng.

"Our class has one guy, two girls."

Wǒmen bānshang yǒu sìge nánshēng, sān'ge nǚshēng.

"Our class has four guys, three girls."

Wǒmen bānshang yǒu liùge nánshēng, wǔge nǚshēng.

"Our class has six guys, five girls."

Wǒmen bānshang yǒu bāge nánshēng, qīge nǚshēng.

"Our class has eight guys, seven girls."

Wǒmen bānshang yǒu shíge nánshēng, jiǔge nǚshēng.

"Our class has ten guys, nine girls."

5. Use the conjunction **nà** and the final particle **ne** to introduce the new topic indicated.

Tāmen bānshang yǒu shíge tóngxué.
(nǐmen bānshang)

"Their class has ten classmates." ("your class")

Nà, nǐmen bānshang ne?

"And how about your class?"

Tā yǒu sānwèi Zhōngwén lǎoshī. (nǐ)

"He has three Chinese teachers." ("you")

Nà, nǐ ne?

"And what about you?"

Wǒmende gōngsī yǒu liǎngwèi jīnglǐ. (nǐde gōngsī)

"Our company has two managers." ("your company")

Nà, nǐde gōngsī ne?

"And what about your company?"

Tāde lǎoshī dōu shi nánde. (nǐde lǎoshī)

"Her teachers are all male." ("your teachers")

Nà, nǐde lǎoshī ne?

"And what about your teachers?"

Tā xìng Chén. (nǐ)

"Her last name is Chen." ("you")

Nà, nǐ ne?

"And what about you?"

6. Convert the following Beijing-style pronunciations to non-Beijing-style pronunciations.

yìdiǎnr

"a little bit"

yìdiǎn

"a little bit"

shìr

"matter"

shì

"matter"

yíxiàr

"(softens the verb)"

yíxià

"(softens the verb)"

tóngwūr

"roommate"

tóngwū

"roommate"

yíbànr

"half"

yíbàn

"half"

yíbànr yíbànr

"half and half"

yíbàn yíbàn

"half and half"

Unit 3, Part 2: Transformation and Response Drills

1. In answering the question, comment that you are, in each case, three years older than your interlocutor.

   Wǒ jīnnián shíliùsuì. Nǐ ne?

   "I am sixteen this year. And you?"

   Wǒ jīnnián shíjiǔsuì.

   "I am nineteen this year."

   Wǒ jīnnián èrshiyīsuì. Nǐ ne?

   "I am twenty-one this year. And you?"

   Wǒ jīnnián èrshisìsuì.

   "I am twenty-four this year."

   Wǒ jīnnián sānshibāsuì. Nǐ ne?

   "I am thirty-eight this year. And you?"

   Wǒ jīnnián sìshiyīsuì.

   "I am forty-one this year."

   Wǒ jīnnián sìshiwǔsuì. Nǐ ne?

   "I am forty-five this year. And you?"

   Wǒ jīnnián sìshibāsuì.

   "I am forty-eight this year."

   Wǒ jīnnián wǔshiqīsuì. Nǐ ne?

   "I am fifty-seven this year. And you?"

   Wǒ jīnnián liùshisuì.

   "I am sixty this year."

   Wǒ jīnnián liùshiliùsuì. Nǐ ne?

   "I am sixty-six this year. And you?"

   Wǒ jīnnián liùshijiǔsuì.

   "I am sixty-nine this year."

2. In responding, comment that your mother is, in each case, six years younger than your interlocutor's mother.

   Wǒ mǔqīn jīnnián sìshibāsuì le. Nǐ mǔqīn ne?

   "My mother is 48 this year. And your mother?"

   Wǒ mǔqīn jīnnián sìshi'èrsuì le.

   "My mother is 42 this year."

   Wǒ mǔqīn jīnnián sānshiliùsuì le. Nǐ mǔqīn ne?

   "My mother is 36 this year. And your mother?"

   Wǒ mǔqīn jīnnián sānshisuì le.

   "My mother is 30 this year."

   Wǒ mǔqīn jīnnián wǔshiqīsuì le. Nǐ mǔqīn ne?

   "My mother is 57 this year. And your mother?"

   Wǒ mǔqīn jīnnián wǔshiyīsuì le.

   "My mother is 51 this year."

   Wǒ mǔqīn jīnnián bāshiliùsuì le. Nǐ mǔqīn ne?

   "My mother is 86 this year. And your mother?"

   Wǒ mǔqīn jīnnián bāshisuì le.

   "My mother is 80 this year."

   Wǒ mǔqīn jīnnián qīshiwǔsuì le. Nǐ mǔqīn ne?

   "My mother is 75 this year. And your mother?"

   Wǒ mǔqīn jīnnián liùshijiǔsuì le.

   "My mother is 69 this year."

   Wǒ mǔqīn jīnnián liùshisānsuì le. Nǐ mǔqīn ne?

   "My mother is 63 this year. And your mother?"

   Wǒ mǔqīn jīnnián wǔshiqīsuì le.

   "My mother is 57 this year."

3. Reduplicate each single-syllable verb and add **kàn**.

   Nǐ zuò.

   "You sit."

   Nǐ zuòzuo kàn.

   "Try and sit on it."

   Nǐ shuō.

   "You say."

   Nǐ shuōshuo kàn.

   "Try and say it."

   Nǐ tīng.

   "You listen."

   Nǐ tīngting kàn.

   "Try and listen to it."

Nǐ xiǎng.

"You think."

Nǐ wèn.

"You ask."

Nǐ cāi.

"You guess."

Nǐ xiángxiang kàn.

"Try and think of it/something."

Nǐ wènwen kàn.

"Try and ask."

Nǐ cāicai kàn.

"Try and guess."

4. Replace the final **ba** that indicates supposition with the tag question **duì bu dui**.

Zhè shi nǐ mèimei ba?

"This is your sister, I suppose?"

Tā hěn ài tā xiānsheng ba?

"She loves her husband, I suppose?"

Nǐmen dōu shi Rìběn rén ba?

"You are all Japanese, I suppose?"

Tāmende fùqin wǔshisuì le ba?

"Their father is fifty, I suppose?"

Nèiwèi xiáojie shi Lín Xiáojie ba?

"That young lady is Ms. Lin, I suppose?"

Zhèiwèi shi nǐ gēge ba?

"This is your brother, I suppose?"

Zhè shi nǐ mèimei, duì bu dui?

"This is your sister, right?"

Tā hěn ài tā xiānsheng, duì bu dui?

"She loves her husband, right?"

Nǐmen dōu shi Rìběn rén, duì bu dui?

"You are all Japanese, right?"

Tāmende fùqin wǔshisuì le, duì bu dui?

"Their father is fifty, right?"

Nèiwèi xiáojie shi Lín Xiáojie, duì bu dui?

"That young lady is Ms. Lin, right?"

Zhèiwèi shi nǐ gēge, duì bu dui?

"This is your brother, right?"

5. Replace the final **ba** that indicates supposition with the tag question **shì bu shi**.

Tā shi nǐ fùqin ba?

"He's your father, I suppose?"

Wǒmen hěn kě'ài ba?

"We're very cute, I suppose?"

Wáng Jīnglǐ sìshisuì le ba?

"Manager Wang is forty years old, I suppose?"

Tā xiǎng qù Zhōngguo ba?

"He wants to go to China, I suppose?"

Nǐmen lèile ba?

"You're tired, I suppose?"

Tā shi nǐ fùqin, shì bu shi?

"He's your father, isn't he?"

Wǒmen hěn kě'ài, shì bu shi?

"We're very cute, aren't we?"

Wáng Jīnglǐ sìshisuì le, shì bu shi?

"Manager Wang is forty years old, isn't he?"

Tā xiǎng qù Zhōngguo, shì bu shi?

"He wants to go to China, doesn't he?"

Nǐmen lèile, shì bu shi?

"You're tired, aren't you?"

For the remaining pages of Transformation and Response Drills
(**Unit 3, Part 3** through **Unit 10, Part 4**),
please refer to the disc.

For the remaining pages of Transformation and Response Drills
(**Unit 3, Part 3** through **Unit 10, Part 4**),
please refer to the disc.

4. Role Play Exercises

. . . .

Unit 1, Part 1: Role Play Exercises

Practice these role plays in Chinese to improve your spoken fluency.

1. A: How are you?

   B: How are you?

   A: Where are you going?

   B: I'm going to the dining hall. How about you?

   A: I'm going to the library.

2. A: Hello!

   B: Hi!

   A: Where are you going?

   B: I'm going back to my dorm. And you?

   A: I'm going to take care of a little something.

3. A: Hello, how are you doing?

   B: Hi!

   A: Where are you going?

   B: I'm going to the library. How about yourself?

   A: I'm also going to the library.

4. A: Hi! Where is Wang Jingsheng going?

   B: Wang Jingsheng is going to the library.

   A: And Ke Leien?

   B: Ke Leien is also going to the library.

   A: And you?

   B: I'm returning to my dorm.

The following role plays use some of the vocabulary from the Classroom Expressions.

5. A: Good morning! How are you? Where are you going?

   B: I'm going to take care of some stuff. How about you?

   A: I'm going to the dining hall.

   B: Good, very good. Goodbye! See you tomorrow.

   A: See you tomorrow!

6. A: Good morning! How are you? Where are you going?

   B: I'm going back to my dorm.

   A: Could you say that again?

   B: I'm returning to my dormitory. How about you? Where are you going?

   A: I'm also returning to my dormitory.

Unit 1, Part 2: Role Play Exercises

Practice these role plays in Chinese to improve your spoken fluency.

1. A: How are you?

   B: How are you? I haven't seen you for a long time. How have you been?

   A: Fine, thanks. How are your mom and dad?

   B: They're both fine, thanks.

   A: I'll be going now. So long!

   B: So long!

2. A: Hi! Long time no see! How have you been?

   B: Pretty good. How have you been?

   A: Very busy.

   B: I've been very busy, too.

   (switch to another pair of students)

   A: How is your spouse?

   B: He/she's fine, thanks. How about your spouse?

   A: He/she's fine, too.

   B: I have something I have to do. I'll be going now. See you!

   A: See you!

3. A: Haven't seen you for quite a while. How have you been?

   B: I've been very busy. How have you been?

   A: I've been very busy, too. How are your spouse and children?

   B: They're all fine, thanks. How are your mom and dad?

   (switch to another pair of students)

   A: They're both fine, too.

   B: Where are you going?

   A: I'm going to the library. And you?

   B: I have something I have to do. I'll be going now...

4. A: Hi! Long time no see! How have you been?

   B: I'm very tired. How have you been?

   A: I'm also very tired.

   B: How is your mom?

   A: She's very busy.

   (switch to another pair of students)

   B: How's your dad?

   A: He's fine.

   B: Where are you going?

   A: I'm returning to my dorm. And you?

   B: I'm going to the cafeteria. I'll be going now...

   A: Bye-bye!

Unit 1, Part 3: Role Play Exercises

Practice these role plays in Chinese to improve your spoken fluency.

1. A: Hi, Old Gao, how are you? Have you been busy lately?

   B: I'm still the same as before. I'm not too busy. Little Wang, how have you been recently?

   A: Pretty good, not too busy. How have your studies been going? Is Chinese hard?

   (switch to another pair of students)

   B: My studies have been quite intense. Chinese is hard! How has your work been going?

   A: My work has lately been very busy.

   B: I have something I have to do, I'll be going now. Bye!

   A: Goodbye. See you tomorrow!

2. A: Hello, Old He!

   B: Hello, Little Zhao!

   A: How have you been doing recently?

   B: Very well, thanks. Still the same as before. How have you been?

   A: Not too well. I'm too busy.

   B: Recently, I've been very busy, too.

   (switch to another pair of students)

   A: How are your children?

   B: They're all fine. Their studies have been quite intense. How is your spouse?

   A: Fine. He/she is not too busy. Where are you going? Are you going to the library?

   B: I'm not going to the library. I'm going to the cafeteria.

   A: I'm going to the library to take care of a little something. I'll be going now.

   B: Bye-bye!

3. A: Hi, Little Wang! How have you been recently?

   B: Hi, Old Ke. I'm very sleepy. How have you been? Are you sleepy, too?

   A: I'm not sleepy. Recently I've been very busy.

   B: How are your studies going? Is Chinese hard?

   A: My studies are very intense. Chinese is very hard.

   (switch to another pair of students)

   B: Chinese is not hard, Chinese is easy! Where are you going? Back to the dorm?

   A: I'm going to the library. Are you going to the library, too?

   B: I'm not going to the library. I'm returning to the dorm. Bye!

   A: Bye! See you tomorrow!

4. A: Little He, you're very tall!

   B: I'm not tall. Old Zhao, you also are not short!

5. A: My father is very tall. Is your father tall?

   B: My father is quite short. My mother is tall.

Unit 1, Part 4: Role Play Exercises

Practice these role plays in Chinese to improve your spoken fluency.

1. A: Mr. Lin, Mrs. Lin, welcome, welcome. Come in, come in!

   B: Mr./Miss Ke, how are you? Thank you!

   A: You're welcome. Please sit down, please sit down. Are you both well?

   B: Thank you, we're both very well. Are your parents well?

   A: They're also very well, thank you.

   B: I have a little something, I must be going now. Thank you.

   A: You're welcome. Take it easy. Goodbye!

2. A: Mr. and Mrs. Xie, welcome, welcome. Come in, come in!

   B: Mr./Ms. Wang, how are you? Thank you.

   A: Please sit down, please sit down.

   B: Thank you, thank you.

   (switch to another pair of students)

   A: Mr. and Mrs. Xie, I have a little something, I must be going now.

   B: Mr./Ms. Wang, where are you going?

   A: I'm going to take care of something. Mr. and Mrs. Xie, thank you.

   B: You're welcome. Take care. Goodbye. See you tomorrow.

3. A: Teacher Zhao, welcome, welcome. Come in, come in!

   B: Mr./Miss Gao, thank you. Long time no see.

   A: Right, long time no see. Please sit down, please sit down.

   B: Thank you. How have your studies been going? Is Chinese interesting?

   (switch to another pair of students)

   A: Chinese is too hard, it's not interesting.

   B: Mr./Miss Gao, I've gotten tired, I must be going now. Thank you.

   A: You're welcome. Take it easy. Goodbye, Teacher Zhao.

   B: Goodbye, goodbye.

4. A: Old Li, how are you? Welcome, welcome!

   B: Little Gao, how have you been lately?

   A: Pretty good. Come in, come in! Have you been well lately?

   B: Still the same as before. How are your spouse and kids? Are you all well?

   A: We're all fine. My spouse is fine. My kids are also fine.

   (switch to another pair of students)

   B: How are your studies?

   A: My studies are very intense. How about you? Is your work busy?

   B: My work is not too busy.

   A: Is your work interesting?

   B: My work is uninteresting. Little Gao, I have something, I have to go now. Thank you!

   A: You're welcome. Take it easy. Goodbye!

Unit 2, Part 1: Role Play Exercises

Practice these role plays in Chinese to improve your spoken fluency.

1. A: What's your name?

    B: My name is ___. What's your name?

    A: My name is ___.

    B: Is he your teacher?

    A: Correct, he's our Chinese teacher.

    B: What is his name?

    A: His name is Lǐ Qún. He's Malaysian.

2. A: Excuse me, what country are you guys from?

    B: I'm Canadian. She's American. What country are you from?

    A: I'm Chinese.

    B: What's your name?

    A: My name is ___. What's your name?

    B: My name is ___.

3. A: Excuse me, are they your teachers?

    B: They're my classmates, not my teachers.

    A: Are they all Americans?

    B: Not all are. This classmate is also American, but that classmate is Taiwanese.

4. A: Excuse me, what country are you from?

    B: I'm American, Chinese-American. How about you? What country are you from?

    A: I'm also American. Are your classmates all American?

    B: They're not all American. This classmate is American, but that classmate is Japanese.

5. A: What's the name of your Chinese teacher?

    B: Her name is Zhāng Huìqiáng.

    A: What country is she from?

    B: She's Singaporean.

    A: How has Chinese been lately? Is it hard? Is it interesting?

    B: Chinese is not hard, it's easy. It's also very interesting.

6. A: Which classmate is Spanish?

    B: This classmate is Spanish!

7. A: Which teacher is named Yáng Pēixīn?

    B: That teacher is named Yáng Pēixīn!

Unit 2, Part 2: Role Play Exercises

Practice these role plays in Chinese to improve your spoken fluency.

1. A: I will introduce you guys. Old Wang, this is Little Li. Little Li, this is Old Wang.

   B: Little Li, how are you? Happy to meet you! Welcome to China!

   C: Old Wang, how are you? Thank you. I'm also happy to meet you.

2. A: Let me introduce you. This is my new roommate, her/his name is ___. This is my old classmate, her/his name is ___.

   B: How are you? Welcome to America!

   C: I'm happy to meet you, Mr./Ms. ___.

   B: Oh, don't address me like that! It's better if you call me Little ___.

   C: O.K. In that case, why don't you also call me Little ___.

3. A: I'm your new roommate. My name is ___. I'm happy to meet you!

   B: How are you? I'm also happy to meet you. My name is ___.

   A: Excuse me, what country are you from? Are you American?

   B: I'm not American. I'm Canadian.

4. A: Who is that?

   B: She is our new roommate, her name is Lìli.

   A: And who is he?

   B: He is our Chinese teacher, Teacher Zhāng.

   A: And who are they?

   B: They are our new classmates. You don't know them?

   A: I don't know any of them. Please introduce them to me.

5. A: Excuse me, are you Chinese?

   B: No, I'm not Chinese, I'm Japanese. Are you American?

   A: No, I'm not American, I'm Canadian.

   B: How should I address you?

   A: Oh, my name is ___. It would be best if you called me Little ___. What's your name?

   B: My name is ___. In that case, why don't you also call me Little ___.

   A: Little ___, I have a little something, I'll be leaving first now. Goodbye!

   B: I must also be leaving now. Goodbye!

6. A: Mr./Miss Zhao, how are you?

   B: Don't call me like that. Just call me Little Zhao.

   A: O.K., in that case you call me Little He, too. Little Zhao, what country are you from?

   B: I'm Chinese. So how about you? What country are you from?

   A: I'm American. Welcome to America! I'm happy to meet you!

Unit 2, Part 3: Role Play Exercises

Practice these role plays in Chinese to improve your spoken fluency.

1. A: How do you do? What's your honorable surname?

   B: My last name is ___. What is your honorable surname?

   A: My last name is ___.

   B: Excuse me, I have a little something (to do). I'll leave first. Goodbye!

   A: Goodbye!

2. A: That must be your husband/wife?

   B: No, no, he/she is not my husband/wife. He/she is my colleague.

   A: Excuse me, I have a little something (to do). I'll leave first. I'm very happy to meet you!

   B: I'm also very happy to meet you. Goodbye!

3. A: I guess that must be Madam Zhao?

   B: No, no, she's not Madam Zhao. She's my Chinese teacher. Her last name is Chen.

   A: Excuse me, I have a little something (to do). I'll leave first. I'm very happy to meet you!

   B: I'm also very happy to meet you. Goodbye!

4. A: How do you do? What's your honorable surname?

   B: My last name is ___. What is your honorable surname?

   A: My last name is ___. Mr./Ms. ___, at what organization do you work?

   B: I work at the Canadian Embassy. Mr./Ms. ___, where do you work?

   A: I now don't work anymore. I study Chinese.

   (switch to another group of students)

   B: Where are you studying Chinese?

   A: I'm studying Chinese at the Chinese University of Hong Kong.

   B: Is Chinese hard?

   A: Chinese is hard, but it's very interesting.

5. A: How do you do? What's your honorable surname?

   B: My last name is ___. What's your honorable surname?

   A: My last name is ___. Mr./Ms. ___, what country are you from? Where do you work?

   B: I'm American, I work at a company. Oh, let me introduce you. This is my husband/wife, his/her name is ___.

   (switch to another group of students)

   A: How do you do? I work at the Chinese Foreign Ministry. Where do you work?

   C: I'm a college teacher. I work at ___ College.

   A: Very happy to meet you! What is your college president's last name?

   C: Our college president is surnamed ___. Do you know him/her?

   A: I know him/her! President ___ is very good. The teachers at ___ College are also all very good!

Unit 2, Part 4: Role Play Exercises

Practice these role plays in Chinese to improve your spoken fluency.

1. A: Hello! My name is ___. Please instruct me more.

   B: My surname is ___. Sorry, I didn't bring name cards.

   A: I didn't bring name cards either.

   B: Mr./Ms. ___, where do you work?

   (switch to another pair of students)

   A: I work at Peking University. Mr./Ms. ___, where do you work?

   B: I work at Sino-American Trading Company.

   A: Mr./Ms. ___, excuse me, I have to go do something. Goodbye!

   B: Bye!

2. A: General Manager Li, this is Manager Xie from China Trading Company.

   B: Oh, welcome, welcome! My name is Li. Sorry, I didn't bring name cards.

   C: My name is Gao. I work at Sino-American University. Please give me more advice.

   B: Mr./Ms. Gao, I suppose that you must be Chinese?

   (switch to another group of students)

   C: Yes, my spouse and I are both Chinese. I suppose that you are Chinese, too?

   B: No, I'm not Chinese, I'm American, Chinese-American.

   A: Excuse me, I have to go work now. I'll leave now before you all. Goodbye!

3. A: Hello! You must be Ms. Bai from the Chinese Foreign Ministry?

   B: You made a mistake. My last name is Hou, my last name is not Bai.

   A: Oh, sorry, sorry, I got it wrong.

   B: Never mind.

   (switch to another pair of students)

   A: I suppose you must be from Spain?

   B: No, no. I'm not Spanish. I'm Canadian!

   A: Sorry, sorry. I got it wrong!

   B: Never mind. I have to be going now. Goodbye! See you tomorrow!

4. A: Who is that lady?

   B: Her last name is Luo. Her whole name is Luó Měiyún.

   A: Who is that gentleman?

   B: His last name is Shi. His full name is Shī Dàpéng.

   A: I suppose they must both be Chinese?

   B: That's incorrect, you got it wrong. Neither of them is Chinese; they're Japanese!

5. A: Let's welcome ("we welcome") Madam Wood from the British Embassy!

   B: Welcome, welcome! I suppose you must be American, too? Oh, sorry, I got that wrong!

   C: You didn't get it wrong. I work at the British Embassy, but I am American.

Unit 3, Part 1: Role Play Exercises

Practice these role plays in Chinese to improve your spoken fluency.

1. A: How many students do you have in your Chinese class?

   B: There are ten—oh, that's not right, I made a mistake. There are nine.

   A: Are they all Americans?

   B: They're not all Americans. There are six Americans, two Germans, and a Frenchman.

   (switch to another pair of students)

   A: How many male students and how many female students?

   B: Four men, five women.

   A: So, how many teachers do you have in all?

   B: In all there are two. One is a male teacher, one is a female teacher.

2. A: Excuse me, how many students do you have in your English class?

   B: In all there are six.

   A: Are they all Americans?

   B: Right, they're all Americans—oh, sorry, they're not all Americans. There's one Brit.

   (switch to another pair of students)

   A: How many male students and how many female students?

   B: Half and half. Three males, three females.

   A: So, who is your teacher? I suppose it's a female teacher?

   B: Correct, it's a female teacher. Her last name is Ramirez. She's Spanish.

3. A: How many classmates are there in your dormitory?

   B: In all there are seven. The dormitory is not big, it's very small.

   A: Are your classmates all Americans?

   B: They're not all Americans. There are 3 Americans, 3 Japanese, and 1 Singaporean.

   (switch to another pair of students)

   A: I suppose your classmates are all females?

   B: No, they're not all females. There are four males and three females.

   A: It's very interesting. Are you going back to your dorm now?

   B: No, I'm going to the library to study. Tomorrow there is a test. I'm very nervous!

4. A: How many colleagues are there in your company?

   B: In all there are eight. Four men, four women—half and half. It's a small company.

   A: So, I suppose your colleagues must all be Americans?

   B: No, they're not all Americans. There are Americans, Taiwanese, and Germans.

   (switch to another pair of students)

   A: Your company's manager is a male or a female?

   B: There's a general manager and a manager. They're both female. The general manager is German, her last name is Weiss. The manager is Taiwanese, her last name is Ma.

   A: I know Manager Ma. She is very good.

   B: Right, Manager Ma is very good. She is a very interesting person.

Unit 3, Part 2: Role Play Exercises

Practice these role plays in Chinese to improve your spoken fluency.

1. A: Is this your mother? How old is she?

   B: Let me try to think. She's forty-six this year—no, forty-seven.

   A: Oh. So I suppose this must be your father?

   B: Yes, he's forty-five years old this year.

2. A: This is your younger brother, right? He's cute. How old is he this year?

   B: He's five years old. Next month he'll be six.

   A: And this is your younger sister, right? She's cute too. How old is she?

   B: She's three years old.

3. A: Is this your older brother? How old is he?

   B: Let me try to think. He's twenty-eight this year—no, twenty-nine.

   A: Oh. So I guess this must be your older sister?

   B: Yes, it's my older sister. She's twenty-seven years old this year.

4. A: You're cute! How old are you?

   B: You try to guess!

   A: Let me try to think… I think you're seventeen!

   B: That's not right. I'm thirty-two. Am I still cute?

5. A: How old are you?

   B: I'll be twenty-one next month. How old are you?

   A: You try to guess.

   B: Twenty years old?

   A: Not correct!

   B: Nineteen years old?

   A: Also not correct! I was twenty-one last month!

6. A: I have neither an older brother nor an older sister.

   B: I have neither a younger brother nor a younger sister.

   A: But you have me, right? I'm also very cute, right?

   B: Right. I have you. You also have me. But you're not cute!

7. A: Let's go back to the dormitory, O.K.?

   B: Not good. Going back to the dormitory is uninteresting.

   A: In that case, let's go the dining hall, O.K.?

   B: Good! Too good!

Unit 3, Part 3: Role Play Exercises

Practice these role plays in Chinese to improve your spoken fluency.

1. A: Excuse me, how much is this bag?

   B: That bag is 50 dollars.

   A: Wow, that's too expensive! How much is this cup?

   B: That cup is only 15 dollars, it's very cheap.

   (switch to another pair of students)

   A: Could I have a look at it?

   B: Sure, why don't you take a look. How many do you want?

   A: I'll buy one. This is 15 dollars.

   B: O.K., thank you. Goodbye!

2. A: Excuse me, how much is that?

   B: That briefcase? Let me take a look. That briefcase is 625 dollars.

   A: Gosh, that's too expensive! Well, how much is that backpack?

   B: That backpack is only 260 dollars, it's very cheap.

   A: Could I look at it?

   B: Sure, why don't you take a look. The backpacks we sell are very good.

   (switch to another pair of students)

   A: All right, I'll buy two of them.

   B: In all it's 520 dollars.

   A: 500 dollars, O.K.?

   B: I suppose it's O.K. In all it's 500 dollars.

   A: O.K., this is 500 dollars. Thank you. Goodbye.

   B: Thank you. Goodbye!

3. A: Do you have backpacks?

   B: Backpacks we have. One backpack is 1,500 dollars.

   A: Gosh, that's too expensive!

   B: It's not expensive, it's very cheap. The backpacks we sell are very good.

   (switch to another pair of students)

   A: How much is this?

   B: That bag is only 600 dollars. How many do you want to buy?

   A: Could I take a look at it?

   B: Sure, why don't you take a look.

   A: I'll buy six of them. How much is that in all?

   B: In all it's 3,600 dollars.

4. A: How much is one cent plus five cents?

   B: One cent plus five cents is six cents.

   A: How much is 90 cents minus 10 cents?

   B: 90 cents minus 10 cents is 80 cents.

· ·

Unit 3, Part 4: Role Play Exercises

Practice these role plays in Chinese to improve your spoken fluency.

1. A: Excuse me, when does the next train to Beijing (**Běijīng**) depart?

   B: At 11:15. But it's now already 11:10, I'm afraid you're not going to make it.

   A: Well, how about the one after the next one?

   B: Let me take a look. The one after the next one is 12:30.

   (switch to another pair of students)

   A: All right. In that case, I'll then take the 12:30 one. How much does it cost?

   B: $28.30.

   A: How long does it take to get to Beijing?

   B: It takes about one and one-half hours.

   A: O.K., thanks.

   B: You're welcome!

2. A: Excuse me, when does the next train to Taipei (**Táiběi**) depart?

   B: At 9:30. But it's now already 9:25, I'm afraid you're not going to make it.

   A: Well, how about the one after the next one?

   B: Let me take a look. The one after the next one is 9:45.

   (switch to another pair of students)

   A: All right. In that case, I'll then take the 9:45 one. How much does it cost?

   B: Fifty dollars.

   A: How long does it take to get to Taipei?

   B: It takes about half an hour. Let me take a look: it takes only twenty-five minutes.

   A: O.K., thanks.

   B: You're welcome.

3. A: Excuse me, when does the next train to Shanghai (**Shànghǎi**) depart?

   B: At 21:05. But it's now already 21:00, I'm afraid you're not going to make it.

   A: Well, how about the one after the next one?

   B: Let me take a look. The one after the next one is 23:05.

   (switch to another pair of students)

   A: All right. In that case, I'll then take the 23:05 one. How much does it cost?

   B: $133.50.

   A: Excuse me, how long does it take to get to Shanghai?

   B: It takes about four and a half hours.

   A: O.K., thanks.

   B: You're welcome!

4. A: What time are you leaving?

   B: I'm leaving at seven.

   A: What time is it now?

   B: It's already a quarter to seven. I'm not going to make it!

Unit 4, Part 1: Role Play Exercises

Practice these role plays in Chinese to improve your spoken fluency.

1. A: Excuse me, what time every day does the library open and what time does it close?

   B: It opens at 7:30 in the morning and it closes at 11:00 at night.

   A: Is it open on Saturday and Sunday?

   B: It's open on Saturday. Sundays it's open half the day; it's open in the morning, not in the afternoon.

2. A: Excuse me, what time every day does the embassy open and what time does it close?

   B: It opens at 8:15 in the morning and it closes at 4:45 in the afternoon.

   A: Is it open on Saturday and Sunday?

   B: It's open Saturday morning. Saturday afternoon and Sunday it's closed.

   A: Thank you!

   B: Not at all.

3. A: Excuse me, what time every day does Sino-American Trading Company open?

   B: It opens at 9:15 every morning; it closes at 5:30 every afternoon.

4. A: What time do you usually get up in the morning?

   B: I usually get up at 6:30 in the morning.

   A: What time do you usually go to bed at night?

   B: I usually go to bed at 11:45 at night.

5. A: How many hours do you usually sleep every day?

   B: I usually sleep seven hours a day. How about you?

   A: I usually sleep five hours a day.

   B: You only sleep five hours? Aren't you sleepy?

   A: I'm very sleepy!

6. A: How many hours do you usually sleep every day?

   B: Monday to Friday I sleep four hours a day. Saturday and Sunday I sleep ten hours a day. How about you?

   A: Monday to Friday I sleep three hours a day. Saturday and Sunday I sleep twelve hours a day.

7. A: Last Monday I was still in China!

   B: Last Tuesday I was still in Germany!

   A: Next Thursday I'm going to Japan!

   B: Next Friday I'm going to Taiwan!

Unit 4, Part 2: Role Play Exercises

Practice these role plays in Chinese to improve your spoken fluency.

1. A: What's your name?

   B: My name is ___.

   A: Which year were you born?

   B: In 1992, it's the 81st year of the Republic.

   A: Which month and which day?

   B: May 16.

   A: Your address is?

   B: Peace Road, Section Three, Lane 5, Alley 8, Number 66, 2nd Floor.

   A: O.K., please wait for a second.

2. A: What's your name? Where were you born?

   B: My name is ___. I was born in Canada.

   A: What year were you born?

   B: In 1987, it's the 76th year of the Republic.

   A: Which month and which day?

   B: November 2.

   A: Your address is?

   B: Beijing West Road, Section One, Lane 20, Alley 4, Number 5, 5th Floor.

   A: All right, please wait a minute.

3. A: Your birthday is which month and which day?

   B: My birthday is June 10. When is your birthday?

   A: My birthday is December 25.

   B: This year I'm 19. How old are you this year?

   A: This year I'm 18.

4. A: What month and day is it today? What day of the week?

   B: Today is ___.

   A: What was the date yesterday and what day of the week was it?

   B: Yesterday was ___.

   A: And what's the date tomorrow, and what day of the week?

   B: Tomorrow is ___.

5. A: What year is it this year?

   B: This year is ___.

   A: What year was it last year?

   B: Last year was ___.

   A: What year will it be next year?

   B: Next year will be ___.

Unit 4, Part 3: Role Play Exercises

Practice these role plays in Chinese to improve your spoken fluency.

1. A: Hello!

   B: Hi! Are you American?

   A: Yes, I'm an American.

   B: Is this your first trip to China?

   A: No, this is my third time. The year before last I came once, and last year I came once.

   (switch to another pair of students)

   B: How long are you going to stay this time?

   A: About two weeks. I go back to my country on November 23.

   B: What room are you staying in?

   A: I'm staying in 702.

   B: Oh, sorry, I have to go now. Goodbye!

   A: Goodbye!

2. A: Hello! I suppose you must be Chinese?

   B: Yes, I'm Chinese.

   A: Welcome to America!

   B: Thank you.

   A: Is this your first trip to the States?

   B: No, this is my fourth time. I came twice last year, once in 1989, and once in 1998.

   (switch to another pair of students)

   A: How long are you going to stay this time?

   B: About a month and a half. I go back on February 15th.

   A: What room are you staying in?

   B: I'm staying in 428.

   A: Nice meeting you!

   B: I'm glad to have met you, too!

3. A: Have you ever taken a train before?

   B: I've taken a train before. And you?

   A: I've never taken a train before.

4. A: Have you ever been to Malaysia before?

   B: I've been to Singapore, but I haven't been to Malaysia. How about you?

   A: Singapore, Malaysia, I've been to both.

5. A: Are you returning home tomorrow?

   B: Yes, I'm returning home tomorrow at noon. How about you? I suppose you're going home also?

   A: I've been too busy recently, this time I'm not returning home.

Unit 4, Part 4: Role Play Exercises

Practice these role plays in Chinese to improve your spoken fluency.

1. A: Excuse me, what's the population of China?

   B: China has about one billion 300 million people.

   A: What's the population of Taiwan?

   B: Taiwan has more than 20 million people.

2. A: Excuse me, what's the population of Hong Kong?

   B: Hong Kong has about seven million people.

   A: Well, and what's the population of Singapore?

   B: Singapore's population is comparatively small. It seems it only has about 5 million people.

   A: Oh, Singapore only has 5 million people?

   B: That's right!

3. A: Excuse me, what's the population of America?

   B: America has almost 300 million people.

   A: What's the population of England?

   B: England has more than 60 million people.

   A: Well, and what about Canada?

   B: Canada's population is comparatively small. It seems it only has 32 million people.

4. A: Excuse me, what's the population of Shanghai?

   B: Shanghai's people are very many. Shanghai has about 17 million people!

   A: What's the population of Guangzhou?

   B: Guangzhou's population is comparatively smaller. It seems it has more than 9 million people.

5. A: Excuse me, what's the population of Xi'an?

   B: Xi'an has about 8 million people.

   A: Well, and what about Taipei?

   B: The population of Taipei is comparatively small. It seems it only has about 3 million people.

6. A: What days of the week do you have Chinese class?

   B: We have Chinese class every day.

   A: Do you often skip class?

   B: I don't skip class.

   A: Have you ever been late for class?

   B: I've been late for class two or three times.

Unit 5, Part 1: Role Play Exercises

Practice these role plays in Chinese to improve your spoken fluency.

1. A: Excuse me, I'd like to find Mrs. Li. Is she here?

   B: Which Mrs. Li?

   A: I'm really sorry, I don't know her Chinese name. However, her English name is Gertrude.

   B: Gertrude? Oh, I know now. Her Chinese name is Lǐ Gē. But, you know, she's not here right now!

   (switch to another pair of students)

   A: Do you know where she is now?

   B: It seems she's now in the general manager's office.

   A: In that case, could I leave her a note?

   B: Of course you can.

   A: Thank you.

2. A: Come in!

   B: Excuse me, I'd like to find Mr. Wang. Is he here?

   A: Mr. Wang? Which Mr. Wang?

   B: I'm really sorry, I'm American, and my Chinese is not too good. I don't know his Chinese name. But his English name is Hank.

   A: Hank Wang? Oh, I know now. His Chinese name is Wáng Jiànjūn. But, you know, he's not here right now!

   (switch to another pair of students)

   B: Do you know where Mr. Wang is right now?

   A: It seems he's now in the college president's office.

   B: In that case, could I leave him a note?

   A: Of course you can.

   B: Thank you.

3. A: Excuse me, if Little Xie isn't there, what should I do?

   B: You could leave a note for her.

4. A: The chairs are here. But where's the table?

   B: The table is over there.

   A: Oh, that's right. Thank you!

5. A: I'd like to buy this chair and that table.

   B: You're only buying one chair?

   A: Yes. How much is this chair? And how much is that table?

   B: This chair costs $200. That table costs $500. In all that's $700.

   A: All right. Thank you. Goodbye.

· ·

Unit 5, Part 2: Role Play Exercises

Practice these role plays in Chinese to improve your spoken fluency.

1. A: Excuse me, is there anybody in this seat?

    B: No, there isn't. Go ahead and sit down.

    A: Do you often come here to eat?

    B: No, I don't come often. How about you?

    (switch to another pair of students)

    A: I eat here often. I come almost every day.

    B: Are you a student?

    A: Yes. Are you a student, too?

    B: No, I'm a laborer. I work at Nanjing Shoe Factory No. 13.

2. A: Anybody in this seat?

    B: No. Have a seat!

    A: Do you often come here to eat breakfast?

    B: No, I don't come often. How about you?

    A: I also don't come often. Are you a student?

    B: No, I work in a trading company. How about you?

    (switch to another pair of students)

    A: I'm a college student in America. This year I'm studying Chinese in China.

    B: Where are you studying Chinese?

    A: At Peking University's Chinese Language Training Center. Gosh! It will soon be 9:00. I have to go to attend class. Bye!

    B: Goodbye!

3. A: I'm a student. I study English at Taiwan University. I suppose you're a student too?

    B: No, I'm not a student. I'm already over 30! I work at a company.

4. A: Excuse me, where do you usually eat?

    B: I usually eat in the college dining hall. It's comparatively cheap.

5. A: Breakfast, lunch, and dinner, do you eat them all in the university dining hall?

    B: Lunch and dinner I eat at the dining hall. I don't eat breakfast.

6. A: Have you ever eaten Chinese food?

    B: Chinese food, I've eaten it very many times.

    A: Do you like to eat Chinese food?

    B: I very much like to eat Chinese food.

    A: In that case, today's lunch, we'll eat Chinese food, O.K.?

    B: That's too good!

Unit 5, Part 3: Role Play Exercises

Practice these role plays in Chinese to improve your spoken fluency.

1. A: Excuse me, where's the bathroom?

    B: It's over there.

2. A: I want to find the bathroom. Excuse me, where's the bathroom?

    B: It's over there—sorry, I made a mistake, it's over here.

3. A: Old Bai, sorry to have made you wait so long.

    B: It's nothing, it's nothing. Old Li, long time no see! You've really gotten thinner!

    A: On this trip of yours to Shanghai, where are you staying?

    B: I'm staying at the Shanghai Hotel, Room 107. Do you still live where you lived before?

    (switch to another pair of students)

    A: No, the year before last we moved to Pǔdōng.

    B: Where is Pǔdōng?

    A: Pǔdōng is to the west of Shanghai. And you? Are you still living in the same place?

    B: In March of this year we moved to the south of the United States.

4. A: Little Zhang, sorry to have made you wait so long.

    B: Never mind. Old Chen, long time no see! You really have put on some weight!

    A: You've put on some weight, too. Both of us have gotten fatter!

    (switch to another pair of students)

    A: On this trip of yours to Tianjin, where are you staying?

    B: I'm staying at the Tianjin Hotel, Room 227. Do you still live where you lived before?

    A: Correct, we still live in the same place as before. We welcome you to come!

5. A: (You) look! That child is really too fat!

    B: That child is too fat? That child is mine. Your children are not thin either!

6. A: Where is my cup? I have to find my cup!

    B: O.K. We'll first look over here, and then we'll go there and look.

7. A: In which part of China is Chéngdū?

    B: Chéngdū is in the west of China.

8. A: Excuse me, in which part of China is Guǎngxī?

    B: Guǎngxī is in the south of China. Guǎngxī is to the west of Guǎngdōng, which is to say that Guǎngdōng is to the east of Guǎngxī.

· ·

Unit 5, Part 4: Role Play Exercises

Practice these role plays in Chinese to improve your spoken fluency.

1. A: Yesterday I bought a new computer. It's in my study. Do you want to see it?

   B: All right! It's a Pentium, right? Inside it, how much RAM is there?

   A: Of course it's a Pentium. Inside it, there are 64 megabytes.

   B: I suppose the switch ought to be in front?

   (switch to another pair of students)

   A: No, the switch is in the back.

   B: Could I see the operating manual?

   A: Of course you can. However, there is only a Chinese one, there is no English one.

   B: Never mind. Where is the operating manual?

   (switch to another pair of students)

   A: It's on the table to the left—no, it's on the chair to the right—I'm sorry, I made a mistake, it's on the computer!

   B: O.K. Hey, what is that thing under the table?

   A: Oh, it's Lassie (**Láixǐ**), our family's dog. Don't pay any attention to her.

   B: I very much love dogs! Lassie, come!

2. A: The day before yesterday I bought a new computer. It's in my room. You want to see it?

   B: Of course I want to see it! It's a Pentium, right? Inside it, how much RAM is there?

   A: Of course it's a Pentium. Inside it, there are 128 megabytes.

   B: Where is the switch? I suppose the switch ought to be in back?

   A: No, this is a new computer. The switch is on top.

   (switch to another pair of students)

   B: On top? That's interesting! Could I see the operating manual?

   A: Of course you can. It's on the bookcase to the right—no, it's on the table to the left—I'm sorry, I don't know where it is.

   B: In that case, I will go look for it. Oh, who is that little kid?

   A: That's my two-year old little brother. Just ignore him.

   B: He's really cute!

3. A: How much does this computer cost?

   B: This computer costs $1,000.

   A: And how much does that computer cost?

   B: That computer costs $1,500.

   A: Both are new computers, right?

   B: They're not new ones, but they're very good. Do you want to take a look?

   A: They're not new ones? If I buy computers, of course I buy new ones! I'm leaving!

   B: Don't leave! Do you want to see our new computers? Don't leave, don't leave!

4. A: Excuse me, was Old Zhao there?

   B: No, Old Zhao was not there, but I left a note.

Unit 6, Part 1: Role Play Exercises

Practice these role plays in Chinese to improve your spoken fluency.

1. A: Uncle, how are you?

   B: How are you, little friend! What's your name? How old are you?

   A: My name is Lùlu. I'm 7.

   B: Lùlu, I guess you already go to elementary school?

   (switch to another group of students)

   A: Yes, I go to second grade.

   B: This is a little present I'm giving you.

   A: Thank you, uncle.

   B: You're welcome.

   A: Mm, it tastes really good!

2. A: Auntie, how are you?

   B: How are you? What's your name?

   A: My name is Xiǎo Míng.

   B: How old are you, Xiǎo Míng? I suppose you already go to elementary school?

   A: I'm five years old. I don't go to school yet.

   B: Xiǎo Míng, this is candy I'm giving you.

   A: I very much like to eat candy. Thank you, Auntie!

3. A: Do you like dogs?

   B: I very much like little dogs. They're cute!

   A: Do you like me?

   B: I don't like you. You're not cute!

4. A: What year in college are you?

   B: I'm a senior. How about you? What year in college are you?

   A: I'm a junior. My younger brother is a sophomore, my younger sister is a first-year.

5. A: Let me introduce a friend to you. This is Little Ma. Little Ma, this is Little Ke.

   B: Little Ke, I'm happy to meet you!

   C: Little Ma, I'm also happy to meet you!

6. A: Excuse me, have you ever eaten Chinese food?

   B: I've eaten Chinese food before. It's delicious. I very much like to eat Chinese food.

7. A: Does she have a boyfriend?

   B: She has two boyfriends. One is good-looking, one is not too good-looking.

· ·

Unit 6, Part 2: Role Play Exercises

Practice these role plays in Chinese to improve your spoken fluency.

1. A: Hi! Are you Chinese?

   B: Yes, I'm Chinese.

   A: What place in China?

   B: I was born in Tianjin, and then I grew up in Beijing. Where are you from?

   A: I'm from Canada. You look quite young. I guess you're not yet 20?

   B: I'm 19. I'll be 20 next month.

2. A: How are you? Are you American?

   B: No, I'm German.

   A: What place in Germany?

   B: I was born in Berlin (**Bólín**), and I grew up in Hamburg (**Hànbǎo**). Where are you from?

   A: I'm from Shanghai. You look quite young. I guess you're not yet 30?

   B: I'm 24. I'll be 25 in April.

3. A: Where were you born?

   B: I was born in New York and then I grew up in San Francisco.

   A: Interesting! I was born in San Francisco and then I grew up in New York.

4. A: Are you married?

   B: I'm already married.

   A: Do you have kids?

   B: We have three children, one son and two daughters. How about you? Are you married?

   A: I'm a college student. I haven't yet gotten married.

5. A: What are you doing sitting there?

   B: May I not sit here?

   A: I didn't say you may not sit there! I asked you what you are doing sitting there.

6. A: Moving is very tiring! Have you ever moved?

   B: I have moved before; I have moved twice.

7. A: What is the food in the dining hall like? Does it taste good?

   B: The dining hall food, in looking at it it looks tasty, but in eating it it's not very tasty.

8. A: Excuse me, what is the meaning of **shémme dìfang**?

   B: The meaning of **shémme dìfang** is **nǎr**. I suppose now you understand?

Unit 6, Part 3: Role Play Exercises

Practice these role plays in Chinese to improve your spoken fluency.

1. A: Are you married? Do you have kids?

   B: I'm married. I have two kids, a son and a daughter.

   A: How old are your children? Are they already in school?

   B: They're still too small. My son is five and my daughter is ten months old, so they're not in school yet.

   (switch to another group of students)

   A: Where do you work?

   B: I serve at Northwest Airlines.

   A: Oh. Does your spouse work also?

   B: He/she teaches at a high school. However, because our children are still small, he/she only can work half days.

2. A: Are you married? Do you have kids?

   B: I'm married. I have a daughter.

   A: How old is your daughter? I suppose she is already in school?

   B: Yes, she's already attending school. She's seven years old and is already in second grade in elementary school.

   (switch to another group of students)

   A: Where do you work?

   B: I work at Southwest Airlines.

   A: Oh. Does your spouse work also?

   B: He/she works at a trading company. However, because our daughter is still small, he/she only can work half days.

   A: This is a small present that I am giving your daughter. It's candy. There are no children that don't like to eat candy!

3. A: Excuse me, what's your name? Where do you work?

   B: My name is ___. I teach at a junior high school.

   A: What do you teach?

   B: I teach English.

4. A: What time every morning does your mother go to work?

   B: She goes to work every morning at 9:00 A.M.

   A: What time every afternoon does she get off from work?

   B: She gets off from work every afternoon at 5:00 P.M.

5. A: Why do many people say that Chinese is hard to learn?

   B: I think it's because Chinese characters are too many. Chinese characters are also hard to write, right?

Unit 6, Part 4: Role Play Exercises

Practice these role plays in Chinese to improve your spoken fluency.

1. A: Do you have any brothers or sisters?

   B: I have one older brother and one younger brother. How about you?

   A: I have two older sisters and one younger sister.

   B: Oh, it's already 9:00! Sorry, I have something I have to do, I'll be going first now. In the future, when there's a chance, why don't we chat again!

2. A: Do you have any siblings?

   B: I'm the oldest in our family. I have two younger brothers and two younger sisters. How about you? Do you have any brothers or sisters?

   A: I have two older sisters and one younger sister.

   B: Oh, it's already 10:00. I have to go to class. I've already been late too many times! In the future, when there's a chance, let's chat again!

3. A: How many brothers and sisters do you have?

   B: I'm the second oldest in our family. I have an older sister and a younger brother.

   A: Where do your sister and brother live? Do they live in America?

   B: No. My older sister immigrated to England. My little brother is studying abroad in China.

4. A: How many brothers and sisters do you have?

   B: I have one older brother, one younger brother, one older sister, and one younger sister.

   A: Do they all live in China?

   B: My parents, older brother, and younger brother live in China. My older sister immigrated to Canada; she got married to a Canadian. My younger sister is studying abroad in Japan.

5. A: Oh, sorry. I forgot to introduce myself. My name is ___.

   B: My name is ___. This is my name card, please instruct me much.

   A: Thank you, thank you. Sorry, I forgot to carry name cards.

   B: That's O.K. Sorry, I have a little something, I have to leave first. In the future when there's a chance, let's chat again.

6. A: How are you? This is my name card. My name is ___.

   B: Thank you, thank you. Sorry, I forgot to introduce myself. My name is ___. I was born in Beijing and grew up in Shanghai. I also will give you a name card.

   A: You were born in Beijing and grew up in Shanghai? Very interesting! I was born in Shanghai and grew up in Beijing.

   B: Right, very interesting. O.K., nice to meet you. Excuse me, I have something I have to do. In the future when there's a chance, let's chat again! I much enjoy chatting with friends.

Unit 7, Part 1: Role Play Exercises

Practice these role plays in Chinese to improve your spoken fluency.

1. A: Where do you live?

   B: We live to the west of Beijing city.

   A: Who all is there in your family?

   B: Me and my spouse, in addition there are two children.

   (switch to another group of students)

   A: Boys or girls? How old are they?

   B: A four-year-old boy and a one-year-old girl.

   A: Where do you work?

   B: I work at a kindergarten.

   A: And your spouse?

   B: He/she formerly worked in a factory. Because her/his health was not too good, he/she now has changed her/his line of work. He/she does a little small-scale business.

2. A: Where do you live?

   B: We live to the south of Shanghai city.

   A: Who all is there in your family?

   B: Me and my spouse, in addition there is one child.

   (switch to another group of students)

   A: Boy or girl? How old?

   B: A son. He's eleven years old.

   A: Could I ask where you work?

   B: I work at a factory.

   A: And your spouse?

   B: He/she formerly taught English in a high school. Because the money was too little, he/she changed jobs. Now he/she works at a computer company.

3. A: Where do you live?

   B: We live in Taipei County, to the east of Taipei city.

   A: Who all is there in your family?

   B: There are three in our family: me, my spouse, and in addition there is one child.

   (switch to another group of students)

   A: Boy or girl? How old?

   B: A daughter. She's sixteen years old.

   A: Where do you and your spouse work?

   B: I serve at the Foreign Ministry. My spouse formerly also worked at the Foreign Ministry. Because the work was too intense, therefore he/she changed jobs. Now he/she teaches English at home. He/she has about twenty students.

4. A: How many people are there in your family?

   B: There are three in our family.

· ·

Unit 7, Part 2: Role Play Exercises

Practice these role plays in Chinese to improve your spoken fluency.

1. A: Hello! You can speak Chinese!

    B: I don't speak it very well, but I can speak a little.

    A: Oh, you speak pretty well! Where did you learn?

    B: At first I studied some in England. Now I'm continuing to study it at Peking University.

    A: Can you also read ("recognize") Chinese characters?

    B: I recognize a couple hundred but I can write only about 100.

    A: I forgot to introduce myself. My name is ___. What's your name?

    B: My name is ___. I'm sorry, I have something I have to do now. In the future if there's a chance let's chat again!

2. A: I know you can speak Chinese; you speak it very well. Excuse me, can you write it, too?

    B: I don't write it very well, but I can write a little.

    A: Where did you learn your Chinese characters?

    B: I learned some in high school. Now I'm continuing my studies of them here.

    A: You know Chinese and English. Do you know any other languages?

    B: I studied French in elementary school and studied German in junior high school. Before I used to be able to speak a little Japanese, but now I've completely forgotten.

3. A: There are people who say Japanese is hard to learn. Do you speak Japanese?

    B: I don't know Japanese, but I can speak German.

    A: Oh, you can speak German. Do you speak it very well?

    B: Pretty well.

    A: Where did you learn German?

    B: My mom and dad speak it at home.

    A: Can you write German, too?

    B: Before I couldn't, but now I'm studying German in college.

4. A: Can you write Chinese?

    B: Yes, I can.

    A: About how many characters have you learned?

    B: I've learned a few hundred characters. About 250 characters, I suppose.

    A: Nice chatting with you. I have to go to class now. Bye!

5. A: Your Mandarin, you really speak it very well!

    B: Not at all, not at all.

    A: How many Chinese characters can you write?

    B: I used to recognize several thousand, now I only recognize a couple hundred. Some I can write, some I can't write. Do you know English?

    A: My English, I forgot it completely! English is very hard to learn, very easy to forget!

Unit 7, Part 3: Role Play Exercises

Practice these role plays in Chinese to improve your spoken fluency.

1. A: When did you arrive in China?

    B: I arrived in the month of March this year.

    A: Did you come alone?

    B: No, I came together with my older brother.

    (switch to another pair of students)

    A: Where did you learn Chinese? Did you learn it previously in America?

    B: Yes. In the beginning I studied it in America. Later I studied for a while in Singapore.

    A: No wonder you speak Chinese so well!

    B: Not at all. It still has a long ways to go!

2. A: When did you arrive in Taiwan?

    B: I arrived in October of this year.

    A: Did you come alone?

    B: No, I came together with two friends.

    (switch to another pair of students)

    A: Where did you learn Chinese? Did you learn it previously in China?

    B: No. In the beginning I studied it in America. Later I studied for a while in Hong Kong.

    A: No wonder you speak Chinese so well!

    B: Not at all. My Chinese is not very good. It still has a long ways to go!

3. A: When did she arrive in America?

    B: She arrived in the month of August this year.

    A: With whom did she come together? Did she come together with her husband?

    B: She hasn't married yet; she doesn't have a husband! She came alone.

    (switch to another pair of students)

    A: Where did she learn English? Did she learn it previously in America?

    B: In the beginning she studied it in China. Later she studied for a while in England.

    A: No wonder she speaks English so well!

    B: Sometimes she speaks so-so, sometimes she speaks not very well.

4. A: When did you arrive in Hong Kong?

    B: I arrived in February of this year.

    A: I suppose you didn't come alone?

    B: No, I came together with my older sister.

    (switch to another pair of students)

    A: Where did you learn Chinese? Did you learn it previously in Canada?

    B: Yes. In the beginning I studied it in Canada. Later I studied for a while in Beijing.

    A: No wonder you speak Chinese so well!

    B: Not at all. It still has a long ways to go! I don't speak Chinese very well, Chinese characters I also don't very much know how to write.

. . . .

Unit 7, Part 4: Role Play Exercises

Practice these role plays in Chinese to improve your spoken fluency.

1. A: Excuse me,did you come from Taiwan?

   B: Yes. Have you ever been to Taiwan? You speak Chinese very well!

   A: Not at all. Where in Taiwan is your home?

   B: Tainan (**Táinán**). It's an ancient city. Have you ever heard of it?

   A: I have heard of it.

   (switch to another pair of students)

   A: Before you came to America, where did you work?

   B: After I graduated from high school, I worked in a factory for several years (A: Oh.), then I applied to come to America to attend college.

   A: Oh, it was like this. So, what do you plan to do after you graduate from college?

   B: After I graduate from college, I plan to go back to Taiwan and look for a good job.

   A: Of course!

2. A: Excuse me, are you from China?

   B: Yes. Have you ever been to China? You speak Chinese very well!

   A: Not at all. Where in China is your home?

   B: **Luòyáng**. It's an ancient city. Have you ever heard of it?

   A: **Luòyáng**, is it? Sorry, it seems I haven't heard of it.

   (switch to another pair of students)

   A: So, before you came to America, where did you work?

   B: After I graduated from college, I taught for several years at an elementary school (A: Oh.), then I applied to come to America to study at graduate school.

   A: Oh, it was like this. So, how do you feel America is like?

   B: America is not bad. America is very wealthy, most people work very hard. It's just that there's quite a bit of crime.

   A: Oh.

3. A: Excuse me, are you from America?

   B: Yes. Have you ever been to America? You speak English very well!

   A: Not at all. Where in America is your home?

   B: New York City. One month ago I was still there. New York is a big city. I suppose you have heard of it before?

   A: Of course I have heard of it!

   (switch to another pair of students)

   A: Before you came to China, what did you do in America?

   B: After I graduated from high school, I worked at a company for several years, but the work wasn't very interesting. (A: Oh.). Then I applied to come to the Chinese Language Training Center at Peking University to study Chinese. I also teach a little English.

   A: Oh, it's like this. So, what do you think of China?

   B: I feel China is very interesting. I very much like it. Chinese food is also very delicious. It's just that sometimes the toilets here…

   A: Oh… You speak correctly.

Unit 8, Part 1: Role Play Exercises

Practice these role plays in Chinese to improve your spoken fluency.

1. A: Excuse me, how do you get to the Shanghai Hotel?

   B: The Shanghai Hotel, is it? Keep going straight, after you pass the library you will have arrived.

   A: Is it very far from here?

   B: It's not far from here.

   (switch to another pair of students)

   A: Probably how long does it take?

   B: If you walk, it probably takes half an hour more or less. Or you take a taxi and it will be even faster; in ten minutes then you will have arrived.

   A: All right, thank you!

   B: You're welcome.

2. A: Excuse me, how do you get to Sino-American Trade Company?

   B: Sino-American Trade Company, is it? Keep walking toward the north for about ten minutes. After you pass the U.S. Embassy, walk toward the south for about five minutes and then you will have arrived.

   A: Is it far from here?

   B: It's not far from here. It's close to here.

   (switch to another pair of students)

   A: Probably how long does it take?

   B: I already said! If you walk, it probably takes fifteen minutes more or less. Or you take a taxi and it will be even faster, in five minutes then you will have arrived.

   A: All right, thank you!

   B: It's nothing.

3. A: How does one get to your home?

   B: First drive east, and then after you pass the Great Wall Hotel, drive west.

   A: Is your home far from the Great Wall Hotel?

   B: My home is very close to the Great Wall Hotel. In a few minutes you'll be there.

4. A: Excuse me, are you from America?

   B: Yes, I'm American, a Southerner. My home is in the state of Alabama (**Ālābāmǎ zhōu**).

   A: I'm also a Southerner, a Chinese Southerner. My home is in Guangdong province (**Guǎngdōng shěng**).

   B: At home we speak Southern speech. Don't know if you understand it or not?

5. A: Where is their Japanese teacher from? Is she American?

   B: I know she's not a Westerner, she's Asian. However, she's not Japanese; it seems she's Chinese.

Unit 8, Part 2: Role Play Exercises

Practice these role plays in Chinese to improve your spoken fluency.

1. A: Hello? Peace Hotel Taxi Company.

   B: Hello? How are you? I want a car to the Peace Hotel.

   A: Where are you now?

   B: I'm at Capital Airport.

   A: How many people?

   B: Three.

   (switch to another pair of students)

   A: When do you want the car?

   B: Right now.

   A: All right. What's your name?

   B: I'm a student who has come from America. My Chinese name is ___.

   A: O.K. The car will be there in five minutes. Please wait at the entrance to the airport.

   B: All right, thanks!

2. A: Hello? Is this the Friendship Hotel taxi company?

   B: Yes. Do you want a car?

   A: I want two taxis to the U.S. Embassy.

   B: You want two taxis?

   A: Yes, there are seven people in all.

   B: Seven people? All right. Where are you now?

   A: We're at Peking University.

   (switch to another pair of students)

   B: When do you want the cars?

   A: In fifteen minutes.

   B: What's your name?

   A: My name is ___.

   B: Are you a foreigner? You speak Chinese very well!

   A: Not at all. I'm a professor from America.

   B: O.K., two taxis will be there at 2:30. Please wait at the entrance to Peking University.

   A: Good, thanks!

3. A: Hello? I want a car to the Foreign Ministry. I'm now at the Great Wall Hotel.

   B: How many people?

   A: Just me alone.

   B: The car will be there in half an hour. Please wait at the entrance to the Great Wall Hotel.

4. A: Why in Beijing are there so many foreigners?

   B: Do you feel that foreigners are many?

   A: Yes. I want to speak the Chinese language with Chinese people! I don't want to speak foreign languages with foreigners!

   B: Your liking to speak Chinese is very good, but don't forget, you're a foreigner, too!

Unit 8, Part 3: Role Play Exercises

Practice these role plays in Chinese to improve your spoken fluency.

1. A: Hello? How are you? New Asia Taxi Company.

   B: Hello, 20 minutes ago I called and requested a cab. You said it would arrive in 15 minutes. How come up until now it still hasn't come?

   A: I'm sorry. We've already dispatched the cab. But it's rush hour now, traffic is very congested. Please be patient and wait a bit longer.

   (switch to another pair of students)

   B: How much longer do I have to wait?

   A: Please don't get excited. I think it's likely to arrive in about 5 minutes.

   B: Please do try to hurry, O.K.? I have to go to the airport to take a plane. Soon I'll be late.

   A: O.K. I'll immediately notify the driver to rush there as fast as he can.

2. A: Hello? How are you? Friendship Hotel Taxi Company.

   B: Hello, one hour ago I called and requested a cab. You said it would arrive in half an hour. How come up until now it still hasn't come?

   A: I'm sorry. We've already dispatched the cab. But it's rush hour now, traffic is very congested. Please be patient and wait a bit longer.

   (switch to another pair of students)

   B: How much longer do I have to wait?

   A: Please don't get excited. I think it's likely to arrive in a little while.

   B: Please try to hurry, O.K.? I have to take a 12:30 train. Soon I'll be late.

   A: O.K. I'll immediately notify the driver to rush there as fast as he can.

3. A: Hello? How are you! Beijing Number One Taxi Company.

   B: Hello? Three hours ago I called and requested a cab. You said it would arrive immediately. How come up until now it still hasn't come?

   A: I'm sorry, it seems we forgot. What's your name? How many people? Where are you now? What time do you want the car? Hello? Hello? Hello?

4. A: I heard yesterday Little Lin waited for a taxi for an hour, but it still didn't come! She was very excited!

   B: When the taxi still hadn't come, what did she decide to do?

   A: She decided to walk.

5. A: Old Zhang, I'm waiting for a taxi, but it hasn't come yet. What should I do?

   B: I know, it's rush hour now, traffic is very congested. Why don't you call the taxi company again?

   A: I've already called on the phone three times! Do you have a way to make them come here?

   B: I don't have a way either.

. . . .

Unit 8, Part 4: Role Play Exercises

Practice these role plays in Chinese to improve your spoken fluency.

1. A: Is it you who wants a taxi to Capital Airport?

   B: Yes, it's us.

   A: Are you American? You're very tall! How tall are you? How much do you weigh?

   B: Yes, I'm American. I'm one meter eighty-five. I weigh ninety-two kilograms.

   A: Only these three pieces of luggage?

   B: Yes, these three pieces of luggage. How long does it take from here to Capital Airport?

   A: Normally half an hour, but now it's rush hour, so probably it will take one hour give or take.

   (switch to another pair of students)

   A: Darn! There's a traffic jam here again. We've no choice but to change to a different road.

   B: Is the airport still far from here?

   A: It's not far, it's close to here. We'll probably arrive in about 10 minutes.

   B: I'll give you two hundred dollars. Give me fifty dollars in change and that'll be fine.

2. A: Is it you who wants a taxi to the Friendship Hotel?

   B: No, we want a taxi to Capital Airport!

   A: Oh, sorry, I got it wrong. Right, right, right, to Capital Airport. How come I forgot? Uh, how many pieces of luggage do you have? Only this one piece?

   B: No, we have five pieces.

   (switch to another pair of students)

   A: Two people, five pieces of luggage? Never mind, my car is big.

   B: These four pieces are all light, but that piece is too heavy. Let's the two of us move it together!

   A: O.K, we'll move it together. It's really heavy!

   B: From here to Capital Airport takes how much time?

   A: Probably an hour and a half, approximately.

   (switch to another pair of students)

   A: Darn! There's a traffic jam here again. We've no choice but to change to a different road.

   B: We probably shouldn't have gone on this road. What are we going to do? Is the airport still far from here? Soon I'll be too late…

   A: The airport is very close to here. In a few minutes we'll arrive.

   B: Cabbie, how much is it?

   A: 95 dollars.

   B: I'll give you a hundred dollars. You don't need to give me any change.

3. A: You said you can teach me how to drive. How come you didn't come yesterday evening?

   B: I did go! I waited for you for a long time, but you didn't come! In the end, I had no choice but to leave.

   A: Wasn't it in the evening at 7:00?

   B: No, it was at 5:00 in the afternoon!

Unit 9, Part 1: Role Play Exercises

Practice these role plays in Chinese to improve your spoken fluency.

1. A: Excuse me, how do you get to the Beijing Hotel?

    B: Sorry, I'm not local, I'm not sure myself. There are two traffic cops over there, why don't you go ask them?

    A: O.K., thanks!

    (switch to another pair of students)

    A: Pardon me, how do you get to the Beijing Hotel?

    C: It's close to here. From here go straight. When you pass the third traffic light, turn right. Keep going about another ten minutes and you'll be there.

    A: Thanks.

    C: You don't need to thank me.

2. A: Pardon me, how do you get to the Peace Hotel?

    B: The Peace Hotel? I come from Shanghai, I'm not local, I don't know either. Why don't you go ask a local person?

    A: O.K., thank you.

    (switch to another pair of students)

    A: Excuse me, are you from here?

    C: Yes, I'm from here. What are you looking for?

    A: How do you get to the Peace Hotel?

    C: It's not too far from here. Go straight from here. At the next intersection, turn left. Keep going about another three minutes and you'll be there.

    A: Thanks!

    C: Don't mention it.

3. A: Excuse me, how do you get to Tiananmen?

    B: Sorry, I'm an overseas Chinese from America, I'm not from here. There's a traffic policeman over there. Why don't you go ask her?

    A: Excuse me, how do you get to Tiananmen?

    C: It's relatively far from here. Go straight from here. After the first traffic light, turn to the south. Keep going another half an hour and you'll be there. It's on your right.

    A: Thanks.

    C: You're welcome.

4. A: What colors do you like?

    B: I like the color red and the color blue. How about you? What colors do you like?

    A: I like the color black and the color white.

    B: Do you feel yellow-colored backpacks look nice?

    A: No, but I very much like green-colored shoes. At home I have many green-colored shoes. Do you want to come to my home to look at my green-colored shoes?

    B: Sorry, in our Chinese class we're having a test tomorrow, I have to study…

Unit 9, Part 2: Role Play Exercises

Practice these role plays in Chinese to improve your spoken fluency.

1. A: Excuse me, what number bus do you take to get to Tiananmen?

   B: Tiananmen? I have to think... First take streetcar number 478, then transfer to bus number 35, which you take to the last stop, which is Tiananmen.

   (switch to another pair of students)

   A: And where is the streetcar station?

   B: Turn to the east at the intersection in front and there it is.

   A: Thanks very much.

   B: Don't mention it.

2. A: Where's the bus station?

   B: You first go straight, and then when you arrive at the next intersection, turn right.

   A: Thanks.

   B: You're welcome.

   (switch to another pair of students)

   A: Excuse me, does this bus go to the airport?

   C: No, but you can first take it and then change to streetcar number 113.

   A: To where do I take it and change to the streetcar?

   C: Let me think... You change at Zoo.

   A: Oh, it seems the bus has arrived.

   C: Yes, the bus has come. Get on the bus quick!

3. A: Excuse me, how do you get to the Great Wall Hotel? Do you know?

   B: I haven't been there in a long time. Let me think… First go straight. When you get to the 3rd traffic light, turn left. Walk for about 10 minutes and you'll be there. It's on your right.

   A: It seems very far. Can one take the bus?

   B: No, but you can take a streetcar.

   (switch to another pair of students)

   A: To where do you take the streetcar?

   B: Take it to the **Měishùguǎn** Station and get off.

   A: Oh, the streetcar has arrived.

   B: Yes, get on quick!

   A: Thanks.

   B: Your welcome.

4. A: I very much like animals. Do you keep small animals at home?

   B: Yes, at our home we keep a dog and two cats. What about you? Do you also keep small animals at home?

   A: Yes, we keep three birds and several fish. The birds can talk! They often say **Nǐ hǎo! Nǐ hǎo!** and **Zāogāo, zāogāo!**

   B: So, what about the fish? What do they say?

Unit 9, Part 3: Role Play Exercises

Practice these role plays in Chinese to improve your spoken fluency.

1. A: Is anyone buying a ticket? Those who don't have a ticket, buy one!

   B: Two tickets to Tiananmen.

   A: Where did you get on?

   B: We just got on.

   A: Two dollars.

   B: Here's the money. When we get to Tiananmen, could you call me?

   A: All right.

2. A: Anybody buying a ticket? Those who don't have one, buy one!

   B: Three tickets to Beijing Hotel.

   A: Where did you get on?

   B: We got on at Zoo.

   A: Six dollars.

   B: Here's the money. When we get to Beijing Hotel, could you call me?

   A: All right.

3. A: Anybody buying a ticket? Those who don't have one, buy one!

   B: One ticket to Capital Airport.

   A: Where did you get on?

   B: We just got on.

   A: $1.50.

   B: Here's the money. When we get to Capital Airport, could you call me?

   A: All right.

4. A: My roommate is not very smart. What's your roommate like?

   B: My roommate is not stupid, but s/he's very lazy. S/he doesn't work very hard.

5. A: My room is not only dirty, it's also a mess. What's your room like?

   B: My room is not only clean, it's also neat. Welcome! Please come in! Please sit down!

6. A: Why are you so angry? All of us hope you will be happy. Don't be angry, all right?

   B: I am happy. I didn't get angry. I'm joking with you!

7. A: You really are too lazy; in the future, you'll have to study harder!

   B: O.K., in the future I'll study harder.

   A: And your room is too disorderly. Why is it that only your room is so dirty?

   B: I'm sorry, in the future my room will not only be in good order but also clean!

Unit 9, Part 4: Role Play Exercises

Practice these role plays in Chinese to improve your spoken fluency.

1. A: Soon we'll arrive, I suppose?

   B: It's still early, there are still two stations. When the time comes I'll call you all… Hey, the next station is Tianan-men, you all should prepare to get off the bus.

   A: O.K., thanks!

   (switch to another pair of students)

   B: Comrades getting off the bus should show their tickets!

   A: Oh, sorry, my ticket, I can't find it!

   B: If you can't find your ticket, you must buy a new one.

   A: But my money, I can't find it either!

   B: O.K., O.K. Never mind. But in the future, you really should be more careful!

2. A: Soon we'll arrive, I suppose?

   B: It's still early, there are still eight stations. When the time comes I'll call you… Hey, the next station is Summer Palace, you should prepare to get off the bus.

   A: O.K., thanks!

   (switch to another pair of students)

   B: Comrades getting off the bus should show their tickets!

   A: Oh, sorry, my ticket, I can't find it! I bought one, but now I can't find it!

   B: You'll have to buy one again. Two dollars and fifty cents.

   A: Today taking the bus really was too expensive!

3. A: Comrades getting off the bus should show their tickets!

   B: Excuse me, I can't find my ticket, what should I do?

   A: Because you're a foreigner, this time it doesn't matter; I remember that you bought a ticket. In the future, you really must be more careful!

4. A: Those several Chinese characters, can you read them or can you not read them?

   B: Those several characters, is it? I can't read them.

   A: And how about these three characters? Can you read them?

   B: These three characters I can read. It's **yī, èr, sān**!

5. A: Litte Li, can you fall asleep?

   B: Because I'm very tired, I think I can probably fall asleep.

   A: I'm also very tired, but I don't why, I can't fall asleep.

6. A: The Chinese that she speaks, can you understand it or not?

   B: She's a Southerner, but I can understand it. You can't understand it?

   A: Sometimes I can understand it, but sometimes I can't understand it!

Unit 10, Part 1: Role Play Exercises

Practice these role plays in Chinese to improve your spoken fluency.

1. A: Good morning! What does the weather forecast today say?

    B: Let me see… This morning is cloudy, in the afternoon it's possible it might change to clear weather.

    A: Right. Now in the sky there are lots of clouds…

    B: Starting from the day after tomorrow, it will get hotter and hotter.

    (switch to another pair of students)

    A: What will be the highest temperature today?

    B: Let me see… Today the highest temperature is 72 degrees.

    A: Huh? It seems that lightning struck! And thunder has struck, too! Is it going to rain?

    B: Man! It's already raining, and it's raining pretty hard, too.

    A: So, weather forecasts are only forecasts and are not necessarily accurate.

    B: That's right!

2. A: Hi! What does today's weather forecast say?

    B: Let me see… This morning is clear, in the afternoon it's possible it might change to cloudy weather. In the evening it's possible it might rain.

    A: Oh. In that case, it wouldn't be very good. In the evening I originally wanted to go see a friend.

    B: However, starting from tomorrow, the weather will get better and better.

    (switch to another pair of students)

    A: What will be the low temperature this evening?

    B: Let me see… This evening the low temperature will be 55 degrees.

    A: Huh? It seems that there is thunder! Is it going to rain now?

    B: Shoot! It's already raining, and it's raining pretty hard.

    A: And that's why weather forecasts are only forecasts and are not necessarily accurate.

    B: That's right!

3. A: Good morning, how are you? What does tomorrow's weather forecast say?

    B: Let me see… Tomorrow morning is cloudy, in the afternoon it's possible it might change to clear weather.

    A: In that case, the weather next week should also be quite good, I suppose?

    B: No! Starting from next week, the weather will get worse and worse.

    (switch to another pair of students)

    A: What will be the high and low temperatures today?

    B: Let me see… Today the high temperature is 83 degrees and the low temperature is 46 degrees.

    A: That's impossible! Huh? It seems that lightning struck! The little cat we keep in our family is afraid of lightning. And there's also thunder. Is it going to rain?

    B: Gosh! It's already raining, and it's raining very hard.

    A: Therefore weather forecasts are only forecasts and are not necessarily accurate.

    B: That's right! Recently weather forecasts have been getting more and more inaccurate!

. . . .

Unit 10, Part 2: Role Play Exercises

Practice these role plays in Chinese to improve your spoken fluency.

1. A: Hey, the weather here is not bad! It's neither cold nor hot, quite comfortable.

   B: Summers are O.K. Winters are incredibly cold, both dry and cold, and it often snows.

   A: Well, what about spring and fall?

   B: In the spring it often rains. The fall is very nice. If you want to come here to have a good time, the fall is the most appropriate.

   A: Saying it like that, I've come at just the right time!

2. A: Hey, the weather here is not bad! It's neither dry nor cold, quite comfortable.

   B: Winters are O.K. Summers are incredibly hot, both dry and hot, and the wind is strong.

   A: Well, what about the spring?

   B: If it weren't that the blowing sand is too strong, it would be O.K. In the spring it often rains. The fall is relatively good. If you want to come here to have fun, the fall and winter are the most appropriate.

   A: Saying it like that, I've come at just the right time!

3. A: The weather there is pretty good, you know! Neither cold nor hot, very comfortable!

   B: The spring is O.K., but the winters are incredibly cold, both dry and cold, and the wind is very strong.

   A: In winter, does it often snow?

   B: No, it seldom snows. However, it is often overcast.

4. A: What are the summers here like?

   B: If it didn't often rain, then it would be all right. If you want to come here to have a good time, then fall is the most appropriate.

   A: If you say it that way, I've come at just the right time!

   B: Yes. Look, the sun just came out!

5. A: The season you like most is which season?

   B: The season I like most is winter. And you? Which season do you like best?

   A: The season I like most is fall.

6. A: The season you like most is which season?

   B: The season I like most is spring. And you? Which season do you like best?

   A: The season I like most is summer. Look, the sun just came out!

7. A: The season you like most is which season?

   B: I don't have any season that I like best. I like every season!

Unit 10, Part 3: Role Play Exercises

Practice these role plays in Chinese to improve your spoken fluency.

1. A: How come there's fog again this afternoon? It seems like it floated in through the window screen.

   B: Yes, this place is often like this in the spring. The air is humid and it often rains. Every day is cloudy.

   A: Actually, it's drizzling right now, but because of the fog, you can't tell.

   B: My luck is really bad. Last time when I came here it rained every day, and I couldn't go out at all!

2. A: How come there is fog this evening? It seems it floated in from the outside.

   B: This place is often like this in the winter. The air is very humid and it is often overcast.

   A: And it often drizzles. Actually, it's drizzling right now, but because there is the fog, you can't see it.

   B: Recently the weather has not been very good. Our luck is really bad!

3. A: The last time I came to Hong Kong I encountered a big typhoon. I hope this time there is none.

   B: Actually, I heard that, after a few days, there is a typhoon that is going to come.

   A: There is a typhoon that's going to come? Where is the typhoon now?

   B: Now it's still very far from us here. Now it's close to Japan.

   A: Dang it! When the typhoon comes, it will rain every day. The wind will also be strong. There won't be any way at all to go outside…

4. A: How come it's drizzling again this morning? There is also fog. It seems it floated in from the window screen.

   B: Yes. Taiwan is often like this in the wintertime. The air is very humid, and it often rains. On the mountains sometimes it even snows!

   A: Actually, it's snowing right now, but because the sun is not yet out, you can't see it.

   B: We really are unlucky! The weather is so bad, there's no way at all that we can go out…

5. A: Little Lin, please go in and look for some things to eat, O.K.?

   B: All right, but how do you open the door? I don't know how to open it.

   A: In that case, please go in through the screen window.

   B: What? You want me to go in through the screen window?!

   A: Don't look at me that way! Of course I want you to go in through the screen window!

6. A: Little Li, how do you get out of this place?

   B: Old Bai, how did you get in?

   A: I don't remember how I got in!

   B: Bye! I'm out of here. You're really unlucky!

· ·

Unit 10, Part 4: Role Play Exercises

Practice these role plays in Chinese to improve your spoken fluency.

1. A: Where in the U.S. do you live?

   B: On the U.S. east coast. Newark, New Jersey. It's not far from New York.

   A: That's interesting! I live on the west coast. So, what's the climate like in New Jersey?

   B: Not very good. In the winter it's colder than Shanghai, and it's also drier than Shanghai. In the summer, it's even hotter than Shanghai. So the climate is not so good as Shanghai!

2. A: Where in China is your home?

   B: On the Chinese east coast, **Qīngdǎo**.

   A: I head the scenery there is very beautiful. What's the climate there like?

   B: Really you can say it's "warm in winter, cool in summer."

   A: Why do you speak in that way?

   B: The weather in **Qīngdǎo** is fantastic. In winter it's warm, drier than here, not as humid as here. But in the summer it is cool, not as hot as here.

   A: In that case, let's all move to **Qīngdǎo**!

3. A: How long have you been in America?

   B: I've been here about half a year.

   A: Well, you've been in America so long, by now I suppose you've already gotten used to the culture here?

   B: Yes, when I first came, I had a hard time adapting. Now I'm just about accustomed to it.

4. A: How long have you been in Macao?

   B: I've been here more than two years.

   A: Well, you've been in Macao so long, by now I suppose you've already gotten used to eating Chinese food?

   B: Yeah, when I first came, I had a hard time adapting to it. Breakfast, lunch, and dinner—I had to eat Chinese food for them all. But now, I'm just about accustomed to it. Now I like eating Chinese food; it's delicious. Have you eaten yet? Come, let's go eat together!

5. A: I most dislike people who arrive late.

   B: Today I arrived 10 minutes earlier than you!

   A: Correct, but yesterday you arrived 20 minutes later than I did!

   B: Really? How come I don't remember?

6. A: My dog died yesterday.

   B: How old was it?

   A: Fourteen. I'm very sad.

   B: Don't be sad, there's nothing that can be done about this.

5. Listening Comprehension Exercises

Unit 1, Part 1: Listening Comprehension Exercises

NAME _____ COURSE _____ DATE _____

Based on the recorded passages, circle the best response to each of the questions that follows. You may listen to each passage as many times as needed.

EXERCISE ONE: QUESTIONS

1. Where is the female speaker going?

(A) To the dorm

(B) To the dining hall

(C) To do something

2. Where is the male speaker going?

(A) To the dorm

(B) To the dining hall

(C) To do something

EXERCISE TWO: QUESTIONS

1. Where is the male speaker going?

(A) To the dorm

(B) To the library

(C) To the dining hall

2. Where is the female speaker going?

(A) To the dorm

(B) To the library

(C) To the dining hall

3. What is the name of the female speaker?

(A) Wang Jingsheng

(B) Zhang Taisheng

(C) Jia Aihua

Unit 1, Part 2: Listening Comprehension Exercises

NAME_____   COURSE_____   DATE_____

Based on the recorded passages, circle the best response to each of the questions that follows. You may listen each passage as many times as needed.

EXERCISE ONE: QUESTIONS

1. How has the female speaker been?

(A) She is fine.

(B) She is busy.

(C) She is tired.

2. Where is the male speaker going?

(A) He is going to the library.

(B) He is going to the dining hall.

(C) He is going to the dorm.

EXERCISE TWO: QUESTIONS

1. How are the female speaker's spouse and child?

(A) They are fine.

(B) They are busy.

(C) They are tired.

2. How are the male speaker's parents?

(A) They are fine.

(B) They are busy.

(C) They are tired.

3. Where is the male speaker going?

(A) To the dining hall

(B) To the library

(C) To do something

Unit 1, Part 3: Listening Comprehension Exercises

NAME_____   COURSE _____   DATE _____

Based on the recorded passages, circle the best response to each of the questions that follows. You may listen to each passage as many times as needed.

EXERCISE ONE: QUESTIONS

1. How has Old Gao been recently?

(A) Very tired

(B) Very nervous

(C) The same as before

2. How are his children doing?

(A) They are fine.

(B) They are tired.

(C) They are busy with their studies.

EXERCISE TWO: QUESTIONS

1. What is the relationship between the two speakers?

(A) Husband and wife

(B) Teacher and student

(C) Colleagues

2. What does the female speaker think about the Chinese language?

(A) It's easy to learn.

(B) It's difficult to learn.

(C) It's neither easy nor difficult to learn.

3. Where is the female speaker going?

(A) Dorm

(B) Library

(C) Cafeteria

· ·

Unit 1, Part 4: Listening Comprehension Exercises

NAME_____   COURSE _____   DATE _____

Based on the recorded passages, circle the best response to each of the questions that follows. You may listen each passage as many times as needed.

EXERCISE ONE: QUESTIONS

1. How are the female speaker's husband and children?

(A) They are fine.

(B) They are busy.

(C) They are tired.

2. How are the male speaker's parents?

(A) They are fine.

(B) They are busy.

(C) They are the same as before.

EXERCISE TWO: QUESTIONS

1. What does the female speaker ask the male speaker to do?

(A) To come in

(B) To sit down

(C) To speak Chinese

2. How has the female speaker been?

(A) She has been fine.

(B) She has been busy.

(C) She has been tired.

3. What does the female speaker think about the Chinese language?

(A) Chinese is easy and interesting.

(B) Chinese is difficult but interesting.

(C) Chinese is difficult and not interesting.

Unit 2, Part 1: Listening Comprehension Exercises

NAME_____ COURSE _____ DATE _____

Based on the recorded passages, circle the best response to each of the questions that follows. You may listen to each passage as many times as needed.

EXERCISE ONE: QUESTIONS

1. What is the nationality of the speaker's father?

(A) American

(B) Canadian

(C) Japanese

2. What is the nationality of the speaker's mother?

(A) American

(B) Canadian

(C) Japanese

EXERCISE TWO: QUESTIONS

1. What is the name of the female speaker?

(A) Ke Jingling

(B) Ke Jinling

(C) Ke Jinlin

2. What is the nationality of the female speaker?

(A) Singaporean

(B) American

(C) Spanish

3. What is the nationality of the female speaker's spouse?

(A) Singaporean

(B) American

(C) Spanish

· ·

Unit 2, Part 2: Listening Comprehension Exercises

NAME_____ COURSE _____ DATE _____

Based on the recorded passages, circle the best response to each of the questions that follows. You may listen each passage as many times as needed.

EXERCISE ONE: QUESTIONS

1. Who is the person that the two speakers are discussing?

(A) The male speaker's new teacher

(B) The male speaker's new roommate

(C) The male speaker's old friend

2. What is the nationality of the person that the two speakers are talking about?

(A) American

(B) Spanish

(C) Canadian

EXERCISE TWO: QUESTIONS

1. What is Zhang Tianming's nationality?

(A) Chinese

(B) American

(C) Spanish

2. Where did this conversation take place?

(A) Taipei

(B) Shanghai

(C) Beijing

3. By what name does the female speaker prefer to be called?

(A) Miss Wang

(B) Xiao Wang

(C) Lili

Unit 2, Part 3: Listening Comprehension Exercises

NAME_____ COURSE _____ DATE _____

Based on the recorded passages, circle the best response to each of the questions that follows. You may listen to each passage as many times as needed.

EXERCISE ONE: QUESTIONS

1. Where does the female speaker work?

   (A) The Chinese embassy

   (B) A company

   (C) A university

2. Where does the male speaker work?

   (A) The American embassy

   (B) A company

   (C) A university

EXERCISE TWO: QUESTIONS

1. Who is the person being discussed?

   (A) Teacher Wang's mother

   (B) Teacher Wang's colleague

   (C) Teacher Wang's wife

2. What is this person's surname?

   (A) Wang

   (B) Li

   (C) Zhang

3. What does this person teach?

   (A) Chinese

   (B) English

   (C) Japanese

. . . .

Unit 2, Part 4: Listening Comprehension Exercises

NAME_____ COURSE _____ DATE _____

Based on the recorded passages, circle the best response to each of the questions that follows. You may listen each passage as many times as needed.

EXERCISE ONE: QUESTIONS

1. Where does the female speaker work?

(A) Embassy

(B) University

(C) Trading company

2. Where does the male speaker work?

(A) Embassy

(B) University

(C) Trading company

EXERCISE TWO: QUESTIONS

1. What does the speaker's husband do?

(A) He is a college student.

(B) He is the general manager of a company.

(C) He is a university professor.

2. What is the speaker's nationality?

(A) British

(B) Malaysian

(C) Japanese

3. What is the nationality of the speaker's husband?

(A) American

(B) Chinese

(C) British

Unit 3, Part 1: Listening Comprehension Exercises

NAME_____   COURSE _____   DATE _____

Based on the recorded passages, circle the best response to each of the questions that follows. You may listen to each passage as many times as needed.

EXERCISE ONE: QUESTIONS

1. How many Chinese teachers does the female speaker have?

(A) Three

(B) Four

(C) Five

2. How many of her teachers are American?

(A) One

(B) Two

(C) Three

3. How many of her teachers are male?

(A) Two

(B) Three

(C) Four

EXERCISE TWO: QUESTIONS

1. How many Japanese students are there in the male speaker's class?

(A) One

(B) Two

(C) Five

2. How many female students are there in his class?

(A) Three

(B) Six

(C) Nine

Unit 3, Part 2: Listening Comprehension Exercises

NAME_____   COURSE _____   DATE _____

Based on the recorded passages, circle the best response to each of the questions that follows. You may listen each passage as many times as needed.

EXERCISE ONE: QUESTIONS

1. Who is the person being talked about?

(A) The female speaker's brother

(B) The female speaker's older sister

(C) The female speaker's younger sister

2. How old is this person now?

(A) 5

(B) 6

(C) 7

EXERCISE TWO: QUESTIONS

1. How old is the male speaker's father?

(A) 63

(B) 54

(C) 47

2. Where does the male speaker's father work?

(A) A company

(B) A university

(C) An embassy

3. How old is the male speaker's youngest brother?

(A) 8

(B) 9

(C) 10

Unit 3, Part 3: Listening Comprehension Exercises

NAME_____   COURSE _____   DATE _____

Based on the recorded passages, circle the best response to each of the questions that follows. You may listen to each passage as many times as needed.

EXERCISE ONE: QUESTIONS

1. What does the female speaker want to buy?

(A) A cup

(B) A bag

(C) A briefcase

2. How much does it cost?

(A) 500 RMB

(B) 520 RMB

(C) 1000 RMB

EXERCISE TWO: QUESTIONS

1. What does the male speaker want to buy?

(A) A cup

(B) A backpack

(C) A briefcase

2. How many does he want to buy?

(A) One

(B) Three

(C) Five

3. How much is he going to pay?

(A) 15 RMB

(B) 40 RMB

(C) 45 RMB

Unit 3, Part 4: Listening Comprehension Exercises

NAME_____   COURSE _____   DATE _____

Based on the recorded passages, circle the best response to each of the questions that follows. You may listen each passage as many times as needed.

EXERCISE ONE: QUESTIONS

1. How has the male speaker been?

(A) He has been busy.

(B) He has been tired.

(C) He has been sleepy.

2. What time does the conversation take place?

(A) About 5:15

(B) About 6:30

(C) About 6:45

EXERCISE TWO: QUESTIONS

1. When is the male speaker going to take the train to Taipei?

(A) 3:10

(B) 3:15

(C) 5:30

2. How long does it take to get to Taipei by train?

(A) About three hours

(B) About four hours

(C) About ten hours

3. How much does the train ticket cost?

(A) 285 NT

(B) 665 NT

(C) 685 NT

Unit 4, Part 1: Listening Comprehension Exercises

NAME_____   COURSE _____   DATE _____

Based on the recorded passages, circle the best response to each of the questions that follows. You may listen to each passage as many times as needed.

EXERCISE ONE: QUESTIONS

1. What time does the language lab open on Saturday?

(A) 8:30 A.M.

(B) 9:30 A.M.

(C) 10:30 A.M.

2. What time does the language lab close on Wednesday?

(A) 8:30 P.M.

(B) 9:30 P.M.

(C) 10:30 P.M.

EXERCISE TWO: QUESTIONS

1. What year in college is the speaker?

(A) Freshman

(B) Sophomore

(C) Junior

2. When does the speaker usually get up every day?

(A) 6:30 A.M.

(B) 7:30 A.M.

(C) 8:30 A.M.

3. How many hours of sleep does the speaker usually get every day?

(A) Six hours

(B) Seven hours

(C) Eight hours

4. When does the speaker go to study at the library?

(A) Monday to Friday

(B) Monday to Thursday

(C) Almost every day

Unit 4, Part 2: Listening Comprehension Exercises

NAME_____   COURSE _____   DATE _____

Based on the recorded passages, circle the best response to each of the questions that follows. You may listen each passage as many times as needed.

EXERCISE ONE: QUESTIONS

1. When is the male speaker's birthday?

(A) August 31, 1986

(B) July 17, 1987

(C) August 31, 1987

2. What does the male speaker do in Beijing?

(A) Working

(B) Teaching

(C) Studying

3. What is the male speaker's address?

(A) 213, Building 14, Beijing University

(B) 321, Building 15, Beijing University

(C) 213, Building 15, Beijing University

EXERCISE TWO: QUESTIONS

1. When did this conversation take place?

(A) March 13

(B) March 14

(C) March 15

2. How old is the female speaker now?

(A) 20 years old

(B) 21 years old

(C) 22 years old

Unit 4, Part 3: Listening Comprehension Exercises

NAME_____ COURSE _____ DATE _____

Based on the recorded passages, circle the best response to each of the questions that follows. You may listen to each passage as many times as needed.

EXERCISE ONE: QUESTIONS

1. When did the female speaker first come to China?

(A) This year

(B) Last year

(C) The year before last

2. When does the female speaker plan to return to her country?

(A) April

(B) August

(C) December

EXERCISE TWO: QUESTIONS

1. What is Li Weijian's nationality?

(A) Chinese

(B) American

(C) Japanese

2. How many times has Li Weijian been to China?

(A) One time

(B) Two times

(C) Three times

3. When does Li Weijian plan to return to his country?

(A) October

(B) November

(C) December

Unit 4, Part 4: Listening Comprehension Exercises

NAME_____   COURSE _____   DATE _____

Based on the recorded passages, circle the best response to each of the questions that follows. You may listen each passage as many times as needed.

EXERCISE ONE: QUESTIONS

1. **What is the approximate population of England?**

    (A) 30,000,000

    (B) 60,000,000

    (C) 80,000,000

2. **What is the population of Shanghai?**

    (A) More than 13,000,000

    (B) More than 15,000,000

    (C) More than 18,000,000

3. **About how many more people does Shanghai have than Beijing?**

    (A) 3,000,000

    (B) 4,000,000

    (C) 5,000,000

EXERCISE TWO: QUESTIONS

1. **What is the approximate population of Hong Kong?**

    (A) 5,600,000

    (B) 6,500,000

    (C) 6,800,000

2. **What is the approximate population of Taipei?**

    (A) 3,000,000

    (B) 4,000,000

    (C) 5,000,000

3. **How many times has the male speaker been to Taipei?**

    (A) About 10 times

    (B) About 20 times

    (C) About 30 times

. . . .

Unit 5, Part 1: Listening Comprehension Exercises

NAME_____ COURSE _____ DATE _____

Based on the recorded passages, circle the best response to each of the questions that follows. You may listen to each passage as many times as needed.

EXERCISE ONE: QUESTIONS

1. What is the last name of the person the male speaker is looking for?

   (A) Wàn

   (B) Wáng

   (C) Wāng

2. Where is the person that the male speaker is looking for?

   (A) At the person's own office

   (B) At Teacher Zhang's office

   (C) At the female speaker's office

3. Where is the male speaker from?

   (A) Taiwan

   (B) Mainland China

   (C) U.S.

EXERCISE TWO: QUESTIONS

1. Where is Li Derong?

   (A) At home

   (B) At his office

   (C) At the manager's office

2. Why did the male speaker call?

   (A) Because he wants to buy 150 tables and 250 chairs.

   (B) Because he wants to buy 250 tables and 150 chairs.

   (C) Because he wants to buy 250 tables and 50 chairs.

Unit 5, Part 2: Listening Comprehension Exercises

NAME_____   COURSE_____   DATE_____

Based on the recorded passages, circle the best response to each of the questions that follows. You may listen each passage as many times as needed.

EXERCISE ONE: QUESTIONS

1. Where is the speaker studying this year?

(A) Chinese high school

(B) Beijing University

(C) Language center

2. Where will the speaker go next year?

(A) Hong Kong

(B) Beijing

(C) The United States

3. Which meals did the speaker eat in the dining hall last year?

(A) Breakfast

(B) Lunch

(C) Breakfast, lunch, and dinner

4. Which meals does the speaker eat in the dining hall now?

(A) Breakfast

(B) Lunch

(C) Breakfast, lunch, and dinner

EXERCISE TWO: QUESTIONS

1. What are the two speakers doing?

(A) Having breakfast

(B) Having lunch

(C) Having dinner

2. Does the male speaker come to the restaurant often?

(A) Yes, often

(B) No, not often

(C) He has only been once

3. How many times has the female speaker been to the restaurant?

(A) One time

(B) Two times

(C) Three times

4. Where does the male speaker work?

(A) At a university

(B) At a factory

(C) At a company

Unit 5, Part 3: Listening Comprehension Exercises

NAME_____   COURSE _____   DATE _____

Based on the recorded passages, circle the best response to each of the questions that follows. You may listen to each passage as many times as needed.

EXERCISE ONE: QUESTIONS

1. What is the female speaker's hotel room number?

(A) 58

(B) 158

(C) 258

2. How long does the female speaker plan to stay?

(A) Half a month

(B) One month

(C) A month and a half

3. What does the female speaker do when the male speaker says she has lost weight?

(A) She ignores him.

(B) She disagrees with him.

(C) She explains why.

EXERCISE TWO: QUESTIONS

1. How many times has the female speaker been to China?

(A) One time

(B) Two times

(C) She has never been.

2. How many times has the male speaker been to China?

(A) One time

(B) Two times

(C) He has never been.

3. Where is Suzhou?

(A) To the north of Shanghai

(B) To the east of Shanghai

(C) To the west of Shanghai

· ·
Unit 5, Part 4: Listening Comprehension Exercises

NAME_____   COURSE _____   DATE _____

Based on the recorded passages, circle the best response to each of the questions that follows. You may listen each passage as many times as needed.

EXERCISE ONE: QUESTIONS

1. When did the male speaker buy the iPhone?

(A) The day before yesterday

(B) Yesterday

(C) Today

2. Where is the iPhone now?

(A) On the bookshelf behind the female speaker

(B) On the table to the right of the female speaker

(C) On the table to the left of the female speaker

3. Where is the instruction manual now?

(A) On the right of the iPhone

(B) On the left of the iPhone

(C) Next to the iPhone

EXERCISE TWO: QUESTIONS

1. Where is the backpack?

(A) On the bookshelf in the study

(B) On the table in the study

(C) Next to the computer

2. Where is the instruction manual?

(A) To the right of the bookshelf

(B) On the bookshelf to the right

(C) On the bookshelf to the left

3. What is the main topic of this dialog?

(A) A backpack.

(B) A computer

(C) An instruction booklet

Unit 6, Part 1: Listening Comprehension Exercises

NAME_____   COURSE _____   DATE _____

Based on the recorded passages, circle the best response to each of the questions that follows. You may listen to each passage as many times as needed.

EXERCISE ONE: QUESTIONS

1. When was the speaker born?

(A) 1993

(B) 1994

(C) 1995

2. What is the speaker's current year in school?

(A) Second year of junior high school

(B) Third year of junior high school

(C) First year of senior high school

3. What did the speaker receive for his birthday?

(A) A backpack

(B) A computer

(C) A bookshelf

EXERCISE TWO: QUESTIONS

1. What year in college is the female speaker's child?

(A) First year

(B) Second year

(C) Third year

2. What do we know about the woman whom the female speaker would like to introduce to the male speaker?

(A) She works at a trading company.

(B) She is a colleague of the female speaker's husband.

(C) She is 26 years old.

3. Based on the dialog, which of the following statements is NOT true?

(A) The male speaker is older than the female speaker.

(B) The female speaker is married.

(C) The female speaker has lost some weight.

· ·

Unit 6, Part 2: Listening Comprehension Exercises

NAME_____   COURSE _____   DATE _____

Based on the recorded passages, circle the best response to each of the questions that follows. You may listen each passage as many times as needed.

EXERCISE ONE: QUESTIONS

1. Where did the female speaker grow up?

(A) Hong Kong

(B) New York

(C) San Francisco

2. How old is the female speaker?

(A) 18

(B) 19

(C) 20

3. How many siblings does the female speaker have?

(A) 1

(B) 2

(C) 3

EXERCISE TWO: QUESTIONS

1. Where does Zhang Guoshu's ex-wife work?

(A) High school

(B) University

(C) Company

2. Where does Zhang Guoshu's current wife work?

(A) High school

(B) University

(C) Company

3. How old is Zhang Guoshu's daughter?

(A) Two

(B) Five

(C) Twelve

Unit 6, Part 3: Listening Comprehension Exercises

NAME_____   COURSE _____   DATE _____

Based on the recorded passages, circle the best response to each of the questions that follows. You may listen to each passage as many times as needed.

EXERCISE ONE: QUESTIONS

1. At the beginning of the dialog, what is the first speaker's problem?

(A) He missed class.

(B) He ate too much food.

(C) He's late to an appointment.

2. What is the problem with this place?

(A) It's hard to find.

(B) It's too expensive.

(C) There are too many students.

3. Why didn't Mr. Bai come?

(A) His children are still small.

(B) He is busy with his studies.

(C) He has things to do at home.

4. What is one aspect of Chinese that the first speaker says is hard to learn?

(A) Culture

(B) Grammar

(C) Computer input

EXERCISE TWO: QUESTIONS

1. What city is the speaker's husband from?

(A) Shanghai

(B) Tianjin

(C) Pudong

2. Where is Pudong?

(A) In the northeast of Shanghai

(B) In the northwest of Shanghai

(C) In the southeast of Shanghai

3. How old is the speaker's daughter?

(A) Ten months old

(B) Five years old

(C) Eight years old

4. Where does the speaker's husband work?

(A) University

(B) Trade company

(C) Airline

Unit 6, Part 4: Listening Comprehension Exercises

NAME_____ COURSE _____ DATE _____

Based on the recorded passages, circle the best response to each of the questions that follows. You may listen each passage as many times as needed.

EXERCISE ONE: QUESTIONS

1. How many sisters does the male speaker have?

(A) One

(B) Two

(C) Three

2. Where did the speaker grow up?

(A) New York

(B) Los Angeles

(C) Guangzhou

3. Where do his maternal grandparents parents live?

(A) New York

(B) Los Angeles

(C) Guangzhou

EXERCISE TWO: QUESTIONS

1. What is the age of the female speaker relative to her siblings?

(A) Eldest

(B) Second eldest

(C) Third eldest

2. Where is the female speaker's brother?

(A) China

(B) United States

(C) England

3. When did the female speaker go to the United States?

(A) Two years ago

(B) One year ago

(C) Two months ago

Unit 7, Part 1: Listening Comprehension Exercises

NAME_____   COURSE _____   DATE _____

Based on the recorded passages, circle the best response to each of the questions that follows. You may listen to each passage as many times as needed.

EXERCISE ONE: QUESTIONS

1. Who are the people in the picture?

    (A) The female speaker's sister and her family

    (B) The female speaker's cousin and her family

    (C) The female speaker's aunt and her family

2. What does the woman in the picture do for a living?

    (A) Factory work

    (B) Business

    (C) Teaching

EXERCISE TWO: QUESTIONS

1. Where does the female speaker live now?

    (A) To the northeast of Beijing

    (B) To the northwest of Beijing

    (C) To the southeast of Beijing

2. Where does the female speaker's son go to school now?

    (A) Elementary school

    (B) Junior high school

    (C) Senior high school

3. Where does the female speaker's husband work?

    (A) Kindergarten

    (B) Elementary school

    (C) Junior high school

Unit 7, Part 2: Listening Comprehension Exercises

NAME_____ COURSE _____ DATE _____

Based on the recorded passages, circle the best response to each of the questions that follows. You may listen each passage as many times as needed.

EXERCISE ONE: QUESTIONS

1. Where is the female speaker studying now?

(A) United States

(B) Mainland China

(C) Taiwan

2. How many characters does the female speaker know?

(A) One hundred

(B) Seven hundred

(C) Several hundred

3. What other foreign language has the female speaker learned?

(A) French

(B) Japanese

(C) Spanish

EXERCISE TWO: QUESTIONS

1. Where did the female speaker learn English?

(A) Elementary school

(B) Junior high school

(C) University

2. For how long did the female speaker learn English?

(A) Half a year

(B) A year and a half

(C) Eight years

3. What does the female speaker think of English?

(A) It's easy.

(B) It's hard.

(C) It's interesting.

4. For how long did the female speaker learn Spanish?

(A) Half a year

(B) A year and a half

(C) Eight years

Unit 7, Part 3: Listening Comprehension Exercises

NAME_____   COURSE _____   DATE _____

Based on the recorded passages, circle the best response to each of the questions that follows. You may listen to each passage as many times as needed.

EXERCISE ONE: QUESTIONS

1. In which month did the male speaker arrive in Hong Kong?

(A) January

(B) February

(C) March

2. How long did the male speaker learn Chinese?

(A) Less than a year

(B) A year

(C) More than a year

3. What level is the Chinese of the male speaker's wife?

(A) Beginning

(B) Advanced

(C) She speaks no Chinese.

EXERCISE TWO: QUESTIONS

1. Where is Nanjing?

(A) In the south of China

(B) In the east of China

(C) In the northwest of China

2. In what level of school is the speaker?

(A) Junior high school

(B) Senior high school

(C) University

3. With whom did the speaker come to the U.S.?

(A) Sister

(B) Brother

(C) Cousin

4. What criticism does the speaker express?

(A) Chinatown is dirty.

(B) New Yorkers talk too fast.

(C) New York is very expensive.

. . . .

Unit 7, Part 4: Listening Comprehension Exercises

NAME_____ COURSE _____ DATE _____

Based on the recorded passages, circle the best response to each of the questions that follows. You may listen each passage as many times as needed.

EXERCISE ONE: QUESTIONS

1. What did the male speaker do after graduating from college?

(A) Teach school.

(B) Go to graduate school.

(C) Work at a trading company.

2. What does the female speaker want to do after graduating from college?

(A) Teach school.

(B) Go to graduate school.

(C) Work at a trading company.

3. What is NOT said about the city of Harbin?

(A) It is cold.

(B) It is a good area.

(C) The people there are nice.

EXERCISE TWO: QUESTIONS

1. How long did the female speaker study in Beijing?

(A) Four months

(B) Six months

(C) Ten months

2. What are the male speaker's future plans?

(A) Go to graduate school in the U.S.

(B) Go to graduate school in China

(C) Study in China for a couple of years

3. What is NOT said about Beijing?

(A) The air is bad.

(B) The traffic is congested.

(C) There isn't much crime.

Unit 8, Part 1: Listening Comprehension Exercises

NAME_____ COURSE _____ DATE _____

Based on the recorded passages, circle the best response to each of the questions that follows. You may listen to each passage as many times as needed.

EXERCISE ONE: QUESTIONS

1. Where should the male speaker go in order to get to his destination?

(A) North

(B) South

(C) Straight

2. How fast can he get to the destination by taxi?

(A) About three minutes

(B) About seven minutes

(C) About half an hour

EXERCISE TWO: QUESTIONS

1. Where is the male speaker's teacher from?

(A) Beijing

(B) North China

(C) South China

2. Where is Harbin?

(A) In the northeast of China

(B) In the northwest of China

(C) In the southeast of China

3. How far is the male speaker's dorm from his teacher's office?

(A) Quite far

(B) One minute on foot

(C) Seven minutes on foot

. . . .

Unit 8, Part 2: Listening Comprehension Exercises

NAME_____ COURSE _____ DATE _____

Based on the recorded passages, circle the best response to each of the questions that follows. You may listen each passage as many times as needed.

EXERCISE ONE: QUESTIONS

1. What is the passenger's surname?

(A) Li

(B) Wang

(C) Zhang

2. Where does the passenger wish to go?

(A) University

(B) Embassy

(C) Airport

3. What time will the taxi arrive?

(A) 5:05

(B) 5:20

(C) 5:35

4. What is the correct romanization for the university that is mentioned?

(A) Fūdàn

(B) Fùdàn

(C) Fùdān

EXERCISE TWO: QUESTIONS

1. Where are the two speakers?

(A) Beijing

(B) Shanghai

(C) Hong Kong

2. How many people are going to take the taxi?

(A) One

(B) Two

(C) Three

3. When will the passenger(s) be leaving for the airport?

(A) 6:00

(B) 6:25

(C) 6:50

Unit 8, Part 3: Listening Comprehension Exercises

NAME_____ COURSE _____ DATE _____

Based on the recorded passages, circle the best response to each of the questions that follows. You may listen to each passage as many times as needed.

EXERCISE ONE: QUESTIONS

1. When did the male speaker call the taxi company for the first time?

(A) 15 minutes ago

(B) 30 minutes ago

(C) 60 minutes ago

2. How many more minutes does the male speaker need to wait?

(A) 5 minutes

(B) 10 minutes

(C) 15 minutes

3. About what time will the taxi arrive?

(A) 5:00 P.M.

(B) 5:20 P.M.

(C) 5:40 P.M.

EXERCISE TWO: QUESTIONS

1. How many times did the male speaker call the taxi company?

(A) Once

(B) Twice

(C) Three times

2. What time is it now?

(A) 10:30

(B) 11:30

(C) 12:30

3. How long does it take to get to the airport?

(A) 5 minutes

(B) 20 minutes

(C) 40 minutes

Unit 8, Part 4: Listening Comprehension Exercises

NAME_____   COURSE _____   DATE _____

Based on the recorded passages, circle the best response to each of the questions that follows. You may listen each passage as many times as needed.

EXERCISE ONE: QUESTIONS

1. How many passengers are going to the airport?

(A) One

(B) Two

(C) Three

2. How many suitcases are there?

(A) One

(B) Two

(C) Three

3. How fast can they get to the airport?

(A) 30 minutes

(B) 45 minutes

(C) One hour

EXERCISE TWO: QUESTIONS

1. How heavy is the male speaker?

(A) 73 kilograms

(B) 86 kilograms

(C) 97 kilograms

2. How tall is the female speaker?

(A) 1.63 meters

(B) 1.79 meters

(C) 1.86 meters

3. The female speaker relates the height of Americans to what?

(A) Trees

(B) Mountains

(C) Sky

Unit 9, Part 1: Listening Comprehension Exercises

NAME_____   COURSE _____   DATE _____

Based on the recorded passages, circle the best response to each of the questions that follows. You may listen to each passage as many times as needed.

EXERCISE ONE: QUESTIONS

1. After passing the third traffic light, where should the female speaker go?

   (A) Go straight

   (B) Turn right

   (C) Turn left

2. How far away is the library?

   (A) 3 minutes on foot

   (B) 15 minutes on foot

   (C) 30 minutes on foot

3. What time does the library close today?

   (A) 7:30 P.M.

   (B) 8:30 P.M.

   (C) 9:30 P.M.

EXERCISE TWO: QUESTIONS

1. Which backpack belongs to the female speaker's roommate?

   (A) The black one

   (B) The green one

   (C) The white one

2. What colors does the male speaker like?

   (A) White and red

   (B) Black and white

   (C) Green and red

3. Where is the female speaker from?

   (A) New York

   (B) San Francisco

   (C) Hong Kong

· ·

Unit 9, Part 2: Listening Comprehension Exercises

NAME_____ COURSE _____ DATE _____

Based on the recorded passages, circle the best response to each of the questions that follows. You may listen each passage as many times as needed.

EXERCISE ONE: QUESTIONS

1. Where is the bus stop for bus 805?

(A) Straight ahead

(B) After the intersection, turn right.

(C) After the intersection, turn left.

2. What bus should the female speaker take to get to the zoo?

(A) Take bus 805.

(B) Take bus 15, then switch to bus 805.

(C) Take bus 805, then switch to bus 15.

3. How far away is the bus stop for bus 805?

(A) 5 minutes

(B) 10 minutes

(C) 15 minutes

EXERCISE TWO: QUESTIONS

1. How far away is Peking University?

(A) 5-6 minutes on foot

(B) 5-6 minutes by bus

(C) 20 minutes on foot

2. What does the woman suggest to the man?

(A) He should walk.

(B) He should take the bus.

(C) He should take a taxi.

3. In what direction does Peking University lie?

(A) East

(B) West

(C) Straight ahead

Unit 9, Part 3: Listening Comprehension Exercises

NAME_____   COURSE _____   DATE _____

Based on the recorded passages, circle the best response to each of the questions that follows. You may listen to each passage as many times as needed.

EXERCISE ONE: QUESTIONS

1. Where did the male speaker get on the bus?

(A) First stop

(B) Heping Hotel

(C) Renmin University

2. How many stops are there before the last stop?

(A) Three

(B) Four

(C) Five

3. How much does the bus ticket cost?

(A) 3.5 RMB

(B) 4.0 RMB

(C) 4.5 RMB

EXERCISE TWO: QUESTIONS

1. Whose room are the speakers talking about?

(A) The male speaker's room

(B) The female speaker's room

(C) The female speaker's classmate's room

2. What is Little Wang like?

(A) She often studies in her doom.

(B) She is hard-working, but not very smart.

(C) She likes to joke with people.

3. What language is Little Wang learning?

(A) Chinese

(B) Japanese

(C) Spanish

· ·

Unit 9, Part 4: Listening Comprehension Exercises

NAME_____ COURSE _____ DATE _____

Based on the recorded passages, circle the best response to each of the questions that follows. You may listen
each passage as many times as needed.

EXERCISE ONE: QUESTIONS

1. What is the male speaker's problem?

   (A) He hasn't bought a ticket.

   (B) He can't find his ticket.

   (C) He can't find his money.

2. At which stop is the male speaker going to get off?

   (A) The Summer Palace

   (B) The next stop

   (C) The stop after the next stop

3. How much did the male speaker's ticket cost?

   (A) 1.5 RMB

   (B) 2.5 RMB

   (C) 3.5 RMB

4. What was the key fact in resolving the problem?

   (A) The male speaker found his ticket.

   (B) The conductor lent the male speaker some money.

   (C) The conductor remembered the male speaker.

EXERCISE TWO: QUESTIONS

1. When did the male speaker come back to the U.S.?

   (A) April 6

   (B) May 20

   (C) June 24

2. Where is Hangzhou?

   (A) In the east of China

   (B) To the northeast of Shanghai

   (C) Quite far from Shanghai

3. When does the female speaker plan to go to China?

   (A) October this year

   (B) January next year

   (C) November next year

Unit 10, Part 1: Listening Comprehension Exercises

NAME_____   COURSE _____   DATE _____

Based on the recorded passages, circle the best response to each of the questions that follows. You may listen to each passage as many times as needed.

EXERCISE ONE: QUESTIONS

1. What will the weather be like this morning?

(A) Clear

(B) Overcast

(C) Rainy

2. What is the high temperature tomorrow?

(A) 31°

(B) 34°

(C) 35°

3. What will the weather be like tomorrow?

(A) Sunny

(B) Drizzling rain

(C) Heavy rain

EXERCISE TWO: QUESTIONS

1. What is the weather like right now?

(A) Rainy

(B) Overcast

(C) Sunny

2. What will the weather be like tomorrow?

(A) Rainy

(B) Overcast

(C) Sunny

3. What is the high temperature tomorrow?

(A) 29°

(B) 32°

(C) 34°

. . . .

Unit 10, Part 2: Listening Comprehension Exercises

NAME_____   COURSE _____   DATE _____

Based on the recorded passages, circle the best response to each of the questions that follows. You may listen each passage as many times as needed.

EXERCISE ONE: QUESTIONS

1. In which season did the male speaker go to Beijing?

(A) Spring

(B) Summer

(C) Winter

2. What are Harbin summers like?

(A) Hot

(B) Dry

(C) Rainy

3. What is NOT true of Harbin winters?

(A) It often snows.

(B) They start in November.

(C) January is the coldest month.

EXERCISE TWO: QUESTIONS

1. What was the weather like last week?

(A) Rainy

(B) Very hot

(C) Neither cold nor hot

2. What is the prediction for the next few days?

(A) It will rain.

(B) It will be neither cold nor hot.

(C) The high temperature will be 78˚.

3. What is the male speaker's favorite season?

(A) Spring

(B) Summer

(C) Autumn

Unit 10, Part 3: Listening Comprehension Exercises

NAME_____   COURSE _____   DATE _____

Based on the recorded passages, circle the best response to each of the questions that follows. You may listen to each passage as many times as needed.

EXERCISE ONE: QUESTIONS

1. On which day did the male speaker return from Taipei?

(A) The 12th

(B) The 26th

(C) The 29th

2. What was the weather like when the male speaker was in Taipei the last time?

(A) Very hot

(B) Very humid

(C) There was a typhoon.

3. What was the weather like when the male speaker was in Taipei this time?

(A) Very hot

(B) Very humid

(C) There was a typhoon.

4. According to the male speaker, which season in Taiwan is best for tourists?

(A) Winter

(B) Summer

(C) Autumn

EXERCISE TWO: QUESTIONS

1. What is the weather like right now?

(A) Light rain

(B) Heavy rain

(C) Sunshine

2. What is Mary doing?

(A) Studying

(B) Sleeping

(C) Having fun

· ·
Unit 10, Part 4: Listening Comprehension Exercises

NAME_____ COURSE _____ DATE _____

Based on the recorded passages, circle the best response to each of the questions that follows. You may listen each passage as many times as needed.

EXERCISE ONE: QUESTIONS

1. Where is Qingdao?

(A) In the east of China

(B) In the west of China

(C) In the south of China

2. What is the winter like in Nanjing?

(A) Cold

(B) Hot

(C) Humid

3. How long has the female speaker been in Nanjing?

(A) Half a year

(B) A year

(C) A year and a half

4. Has she gotten used to the climate in Nanjing?

(A) Yes, she has.

(B) No, she hasn't.

(C) Not at first, but now she has just about gotten accustomed to it.

EXERCISE TWO: QUESTIONS

1. When did the female speaker come?

(A) Around 5:40

(B) Around 6:00

(C) Around 6:20

2. How did the male speaker come?

(A) By bus

(B) By taxi

(C) On foot

3. What did the female speaker's experience show?

(A) Taxi is faster than bus.

(B) Walking can be faster than bus or taxi.

(C) Taxi is not necessarily faster than bus.

4. How would the male speaker's attitude toward the female speaker be best described?

(A) He is angry at her.

(B) He is used to her.

(C) He likes her very much.

6. Dictation Exercises

. . . .

Dictation Exercise 1

PRONUNCIATION AND ROMANIZATION: INITIALS

NAME_____ COURSE _____ DATE _____

Based on the recording for this exercise, write in the correct Pinyin initials. The finals and tones are indicated. You may listen to the recording as many times as needed..

1. _____ā	11. _____ēn	21. _____uē
2. _____ū	12. _____uī	22. _____ēng
3. _____ī	13. _____ān	23. _____ōng
4. _____ō	14. _____ū	24. _____uān
5. _____āi	15. _____ū	25. _____uān
6. _____iā	16. _____ē	26. _____āng
7. _____ōu	17. _____ā	27. _____uī
8. _____āo	18. _____ī	28. _____ā
9. _____iē	19. _____ī	29. _____āo
10. _____īn	20. _____iān	30. _____ī

. . . .

Dictation Exercise 2

PRONUNCIATION AND ROMANIZATION: FINALS

NAME_____   COURSE _____   DATE _____

Based on the recording for this exercise, write in the correct Pinyin finals, which are all in Tone One. The initia
are indicated. You may listen to the recording as many times as needed.

1. f_____   11. r_____   21. y_____

2. j_____   12. g_____   22. z_____

3. t_____   13. w_____   23. q_____

4. x_____   14. l_____   24. r_____

5. j_____   15. zh_____   25. n_____

6. c_____   16. b_____   26. j_____

7. sh_____   17. x_____   27. q_____

8. y_____   18. m_____   28. s_____

9. z_____   19. k_____   29. z_____

10. ch_____   20. p_____   30. zh_____

Dictation Exercise 3

PRONUNCIATION AND ROMANIZATION: TONES

NAME_____ COURSE _____ DATE _____

Based on the recording for this exercise, add the correct Pinyin tones. The initials and finals are indicated. You may listen to the recording as many times as needed.

1. ta	11. zhi	21. xue
2. ma	12. shu	22. lan
3. wo	13. tan	23. mai
4. shei	14. lü	24. mai
5. hao	15. lu	25. pai
6. lei	16. ru	26. er
7. sha	17. rou	27. xiu
8. gui	18. lüe	28. shuo
9. ni	19. ku	29. kuang
10. mei	20. li	30. feng

· ·

Dictation Exercise 4

PRONUNCIATION AND ROMANIZATION: INITIALS, FINALS, AND TONES

NAME_____   COURSE _____   DATE _____

Based on the recording for this exercise, write the initial, final, and tone for the syllables you hear. You may listen to the recording as many times as needed.

1. _____

2. _____

3. _____

4. _____

5. _____

6. _____

7. _____

8. _____

9. _____

10. _____

11. _____

12. _____

13. _____

14. _____

15. _____

16. _____

17. _____

18. _____

19. _____

20. _____

21. _____

22. _____

23. _____

24. _____

25. _____

26. _____

27. _____

28. _____

29. _____

30. _____

Dictation Exercise 5

CLASSROOM EXPRESSIONS 1–32

NAME_____   COURSE_____   DATE_____

Based on the recording for this exercise, write below the English equivalents for the Chinese expressions you hear. Note that some of the classroom expressions from the textbook have here been combined or slightly rearranged. You may listen to the recording as many times as needed.

1. _____

2. _____

3. _____

4. _____

5. _____

6. _____

7. _____

8. _____

9. _____

10. _____

11. _____

12. _____

13. _____

14. _____

15. _____

16. _____

17. _____

18. _____

19. _____

20. _____

. . . .

Dictation Exercise 6

UNIT 3, PART 2: NUMBERS 1–99 AND AGES

NAME_____   COURSE _____   DATE _____

Based on the recording for this exercise, write the number or age that you hear (in the case of ages, write "_
years old"). You may listen to the recording as many times as needed.

1. _____   11. _____   21. _____

2. _____   12. _____   22. _____

3. _____   13. _____   23. _____

4. _____   14. _____   24. _____

5. _____   15. _____   25. _____

6. _____   16. _____   26. _____

7. _____   17. _____   27. _____

8. _____   18. _____   28. _____

9. _____   19. _____   29. _____

10. _____   20. _____   30. _____

. . . .

Dictation Exercise 7

UNIT 3, PART 3: NUMBERS 1–9,999 AND MONEY AMOUNTS

NAME_____ COURSE _____ DATE _____

Based on the recording for this exercise, write the number or money amount that you hear (in the case of money amounts, assume it is American money and indicate $ or ¢ as appropriate). You may listen to the recording as many times as needed.

1. _____   11. _____   21. _____

2. _____   12. _____   22. _____

3. _____   13. _____   23. _____

4. _____   14. _____   24. _____

5. _____   15. _____   25. _____

6. _____   16. _____   26. _____

7. _____   17. _____   27. _____

8. _____   18. _____   28. _____

9. _____   19. _____   29. _____

10. _____   20. _____   30. _____

Dictation Exercise 8

UNIT 3, PART 4: CLOCK TIMES AND AMOUNTS OF TIME

NAME_____ COURSE _____ DATE _____

Based on the recording for this exercise, write the clock time or amount of time that you hear. (Write clock tim
as hour followed by minutes, e.g., "5:35"; indicate amounts of time with "hours" or "minutes", e.g., "2 hours" or "
minutes.") You may listen to the recording as many times as needed.

1. _____

2. _____

3. _____

4. _____

5. _____

6. _____

7. _____

8. _____

9. _____

10. _____

11. _____

12. _____

13. _____

14. _____

15. _____

16. _____

17. _____

18. _____

19. _____

20. _____

21. _____

22. _____

23. _____

24. _____

25. _____

26. _____

27. _____

28. _____

29. _____

30. _____

. . . .

Dictation Exercise 9

UNIT 4, PART 2: DATES

NAME_____   COURSE _____   DATE _____

Based on the recording for this exercise, write the date that you hear, including day of the week, month, day of the month, and year. For example, if you hear the Chinese for "Monday, July 4, 2011," then write below in this order and with these abbreviations: "Mon., 7/4/2011." You may listen to the recording as many times as needed.

1. _____

2. _____

3. _____

4. _____

5. _____

6. _____

7. _____

8. _____

9. _____

10. _____

11. _____

12. _____

13. _____

14. _____

15. _____

16. _____

17. _____

18. _____

19. _____

20. _____

Dictation Exercise 10

UNIT 4, PART 4: LARGE NUMBERS

NAME_____ COURSE _____ DATE _____

Based on the recording for this exercise, write numerically the number that you hear as it would be written in the U.S. For example, for "one billion three hundred million," write "1,300,000,000." If the Chinese uses **duō** to indicate "more than," then use a plus mark (+) after the number. You may listen to the recording as many times as needed.

1. _____

2. _____

3. _____

4. _____

5. _____

6. _____

7. _____

8. _____

9. _____

10. _____

11. _____

12. _____

13. _____

14. _____

15. _____

16. _____

17. _____

18. _____

19. _____

20. _____

21. _____

22. _____

23. _____

24. _____

25. _____

26. _____

27. _____

28. _____

29. _____

30. _____

. Translation Exercises, Units 1–10: For Each Part (Lesson)

. . . .

Unit 1, Part 1: Translation Exercise

NAME_____ COURSE _____ DATE _____

Translate the following sentences into Pinyin romanization with correct tone marks. If you have forgotten a word, consult the English-Chinese Glossary in the back of your textbook.

1. Where is Ke Leien going?

2. I'm going to the cafeteria. How about you?

3. Wang Jingsheng is going back to the dorm.

4. Ke Leien is going to take care of some things.

5. You're going to the library; I also am going to the library.

Unit 1, Part 2: Translation Exercise

NAME_____   COURSE _____   DATE _____

Translate the following sentences into Pinyin romanization with correct tone marks. If you have forgotten a wo
consult the English-Chinese Glossary in the back of your textbook.

1. I'm tired; are you tired, too?

2. Haven't seen you for a long time! Are you busy?

3. He is busy; his wife and children are also all busy.

4. How have your mom and dad been? Are they both well?

5. She has a little something (she has to do); I also have a little something (I have to do).

Unit 1, Part 3: Translation Exercise

NAME_____ COURSE _____ DATE _____

Translate the following sentences into Pinyin romanization with correct tone marks. If you have forgotten a word, consult the English-Chinese Glossary in the back of your textbook.

1. Chinese is not hard; Chinese is easy!

2. Little Wang, hi! How have you been lately?

3. Recently her studies have not been too intense.

4. Recently we have all been quite busy. (use **tǐng...-de** pattern)

5. Is Old Zhao going? Are you going? (use affirmative-negative question pattern)

· ·

Unit 1, Part 4: Translation Exercise

NAME_____   COURSE _____   DATE _____

Translate the following sentences into Pinyin romanization with correct tone marks. If you have forgotten a wo
consult the English-Chinese Glossary in the back of your textbook.

1. Teacher Wang, please come in! Please sit down!

2. We've gotten tired. Have you (plural) **gotten tired, too?**

3. A: Ms. Gao, thank you! B: You're welcome. Take care!

4. Mr. Li, how are you? Mrs. Li, how are you? (be as polite as possible)

5. Miss Lin, I have a little something (I have to do); I must be going now. Goodbye!

Unit 2, Part 1: Translation Exercise

NAME_____ COURSE _____ DATE _____

Translate the following sentences into Pinyin romanization with correct tone marks. If you have forgotten a word, consult the English-Chinese Glossary in the back of your textbook.

1. She is American, Chinese-American. How about you?

2. Are both of you Chinese? And how about that classmate?

3. Excuse me, what country are you from? Are you Japanese? (be polite)

4. I'm called (write your own Chinese surname and given name). **What's your name?**

5. They're not all good fathers. This teacher is a good father, but that teacher isn't a good father.

Unit 2, Part 2: Translation Exercise

NAME_____ COURSE _____ DATE _____

Translate the following sentences into Pinyin romanization with correct tone marks. If you have forgotten a wo
consult the English-Chinese Glossary in the back of your textbook.

1. We welcome you to come to America! (be polite)

2. Who is your (plural) **teacher? Who are your classmates?**

3. Welcome! Please come in, please sit down. Don't leave!

4. I'm happy to meet you. Excuse me, how should I address you?

5. Don't address me like this. It would be better if you called me Little Gao.

Unit 2, Part 3: Translation Exercise

NAME_____ COURSE _____ DATE _____

Translate the following sentences into Pinyin romanization with correct tone marks. If you have forgotten a word, consult the English-Chinese Glossary in the back of your textbook.

1. I study at Taiwan University; where do you study?

2. This person must be your spouse, I suppose? (be polite)

3. My mother works at a company. Where does your mother work?

4. Mr. Wu works at the Foreign Ministry, Mrs. Wu works at the Japanese Embassy.

5. What is your last name? At which organization do you work? (be as polite as you can)

. . . .

Unit 2, Part 4: Translation Exercise

NAME_____ COURSE _____ DATE _____

Translate the following sentences into Pinyin romanization with correct tone marks. If you have forgotten a wo
consult the English-Chinese Glossary in the back of your textbook.

1. Sorry, I didn't go, I also didn't ask.

2. None of them went to the dining hall.

3. A: Have they come? B: They still haven't come.

4. Not all of them are Chinese, but none of us are Canadians.

5. Miss Wang from the Chinese Embassy has come. Do you know her?

Unit 3, Part 1: Translation Exercise

NAME_____ COURSE _____ DATE _____

Translate the following sentences into Pinyin romanization with correct tone marks. If you have forgotten a word, consult the English-Chinese Glossary in the back of your textbook.

1. We in the class have nine classmates. (be polite)

2. You guys in all have how many Chinese language teachers?

3. One is a male student, eight are female students. (no need to be polite)

4. In the class there are seven French people, six Chinese people, and four Germans.

5. There are five teachers; two are male teachers, three are female teachers. (be polite)

Unit 3, Part 2: Translation Exercise

NAME_____   COURSE _____   DATE _____

Translate the following sentences into Pinyin romanization with correct tone marks. If you have forgotten a wo[...]
consult the English-Chinese Glossary in the back of your textbook.

1. How old is their child?

2. Next month I'll be 19 years old.

3. How old is your mother this year?

4. You don't have an older brother, right?

5. Let me try to think: My father is 61 this year.

Unit 3, Part 3: Translation Exercise

NAME_____ COURSE _____ DATE _____

Translate the following sentences into Pinyin romanization with correct tone marks. If you have forgotten a word, consult the English-Chinese Glossary in the back of your textbook.

1. Why don't we buy one, too?

2. How much does that backpack cost?

3. The cups and bags she sells are all too expensive.

4. Why don't you take a look. This is very good, also very inexpensive.

5. This briefcase costs three thousand four hundred and fifty-nine dollars.

· ·

Unit 3, Part 4: Translation Exercise

NAME_____ COURSE _____ DATE _____

Translate the following sentences into Pinyin romanization with correct tone marks. If you have forgotten a wo
consult the English-Chinese Glossary in the back of your textbook.

1. In that case, I then will take the 10:00 train.

2. We will take the 9:30 one. How about you?

3. To Tianjin it takes about one and one-half hours.

4. Excuse me, how long does it take to get to Singapore?

5. Now it's already 2:30; I'm afraid you guys are not going to make it.

Unit 4, Part 1: Translation Exercise

NAME_____ COURSE _____ DATE _____

Translate the following sentences into Pinyin romanization with correct tone marks. If you have forgotten a word, consult the English-Chinese Glossary in the back of your textbook.

1. Excuse me, is the library open on Sunday?

2. I ordinarily sleep seven hours every day. How about you?

3. Monday, Wednesday, Friday the company is open half the day.

4. I usually get up at 7:00 in the morning and go to sleep at 11:00 at night.

5. The language lab opens at 9:00 in the morning, and closes at 8:30 in the evening.

· ·

Unit 4, Part 2: Translation Exercise

NAME_____ COURSE _____ DATE _____

Translate the following sentences into Pinyin romanization with correct tone marks. If you have forgotten a wo
consult the English-Chinese Glossary in the back of your textbook.

1. Her mother's birthday is November 24.

2. His father was born on September 19, 1965 in England.

3. What is the date tomorrow and what day of the week is it?

4. My address is Peace Road, Section 3, Lane 46, Alley 5, Number 27, 7th floor.

**5. How many days? One day! How many weeks? Two weeks! How many months? Three months! How man
years? Four years!**

Unit 4, Part 3: Translation Exercise

NAME_____ COURSE_____ DATE_____

Translate the following sentences into Pinyin romanization with correct tone marks. If you have forgotten a word, consult the English-Chinese Glossary in the back of your textbook.

1. This is my third time in China.

2. Teacher Wang this year went twice.

3. On November 25th I'll be going home.

4. I've never been (= "gone") to China before. Have you been there before?

5. A: How long will you be staying? B: This time I want to stay one month.

Unit 4, Part 4: Translation Exercise

NAME_____ COURSE _____ DATE _____

Translate the following sentences into Pinyin romanization with correct tone marks. If you have forgotten a wo
consult the English-Chinese Glossary in the back of your textbook.

1. How many people are there in Shanghai?

2. Taiwan has about twenty-four million people.

3. It seems Taipei only has three million people.

4. It seems Guangzhou has more than twelve million people.

5. Guangzhou's population is comparatively larger. (use **duō** "be many, much")

Unit 5, Part 1: Translation Exercise

NAME_____   COURSE _____   DATE _____

Translate the following sentences into Pinyin romanization with correct tone marks. If you have forgotten a word, consult the English-Chinese Glossary in the back of your textbook.

1. Where is that table?

2. Do you know where that chair is?

3. Excuse me, is Ms. Zhang present?

4. If I'm not there, can you leave me a note?

5. Mrs. Zhang is here, but Ms. Zhang is not here now.

Unit 5, Part 2: Translation Exercise

NAME_____   COURSE _____   DATE _____

Translate the following sentences into Pinyin romanization with correct tone marks. If you have forgotten a wo
consult the English-Chinese Glossary in the back of your textbook.

1. I work there.

2. Where do you eat breakfast?

3. We often come here to eat Chinese food.

4. She is studying Chinese language at Beijing University.

5. Gosh! Soon it will be seven o'clock. I have to go eat dinner!

Unit 5, Part 3: Translation Exercise

NAME_____ COURSE _____ DATE _____

Translate the following sentences into Pinyin romanization with correct tone marks. If you have forgotten a word, consult the English-Chinese Glossary in the back of your textbook.

1. Shanghai is in the east of China.

2. The year before last they moved to Chengdu.

3. Little Li, you really have gotten a little fatter!

4. I'm looking for the toilet; excuse me, where's the toilet?

5. This time I'm staying at the Beijing Hotel. Where do you live?

Unit 5, Part 4: Translation Exercise

NAME_____ COURSE _____ DATE _____

Translate the following sentences into Pinyin romanization with correct tone marks. If you have forgotten a wo
consult the English-Chinese Glossary in the back of your textbook.

1. In the cup there are five cents.

2. The computer is on that table to your right.

3. The switch is not in the front, it's in the back.

4. That thing that is on top—don't concern yourself with it!

5. Little Wang is outside the library; he's not inside the library.

Unit 6, Part 1: Translation Exercise

NAME_____   COURSE _____   DATE _____

Translate the following sentences into Pinyin romanization with correct tone marks. If you have forgotten a word, consult the English-Chinese Glossary in the back of your textbook.

1. That is the candy that she gave me.

2. Auntie, let me introduce a friend to you.

3. The dining hall food is not very good to eat.

4. This is a little present that I'm giving you. (be polite)

5. Her boyfriend is already in his senior year; he's quite good-looking.

Unit 6, Part 2: Translation Exercise

NAME_____ COURSE _____ DATE _____

Translate the following sentences into Pinyin romanization with correct tone marks. If you have forgotten a wo
consult the English-Chinese Glossary in the back of your textbook.

1. Little Jin, you look very sleepy!

2. I'm not yet married. Are you married?

3. Excuse me, what does qiānzhèng mean?

4. Old Sun, I suppose you're not yet fifty years old?

5. My Chinese friend was born in Tianjin and then grew up in Beijing.

Unit 6, Part 3: Translation Exercise

NAME_____ COURSE _____ DATE _____

Translate the following sentences into Pinyin romanization with correct tone marks. If you have forgotten a word, consult the English-Chinese Glossary in the back of your textbook.

1. That child is six months old.

2. Why do you only work half the day?

3. Do you like to teach? What do you teach?

4. Because we're very busy, we didn't wait for him.

5. You work at Northeast Airlines, right? When do you go to work and when do you get off from work?

· ·

Unit 6, Part 4: Translation Exercise

NAME_____ COURSE _____ DATE _____

Translate the following sentences into Pinyin romanization with correct tone marks. If you have forgotten a wo
consult the English-Chinese Glossary in the back of your textbook.

1. He's the oldest in their family.

2. Sorry, I forgot to introduce myself.

3. Mrs. Zhang, in the future if there is an opportunity, let's chat again!

4. I have one older sister and one younger brother. How many siblings do you have?

5. My older brother is studying abroad in Japan; my younger sister immigrated to France.

Unit 7, Part 1: Translation Exercise

NAME_____   COURSE _____   DATE _____

Translate the following sentences into Pinyin romanization with correct tone marks. If you have forgotten a word, consult the English-Chinese Glossary in the back of your textbook.

1. Who all is there in their family?

2. My parents used to work in a factory. ("used to" = "formerly")

3. Formerly I sold computers; now I've changed my line of work.

4. She works in a kindergarten; she has to go to work at 7:00 in the morning.

5. Because his health is not too good, therefore he now is not engaged in business anymore.

. . . .

Unit 7, Part 2: Translation Exercise

NAME_____   COURSE _____   DATE _____

Translate the following sentences into Pinyin romanization with correct tone marks. If you have forgotten a wo
consult the English-Chinese Glossary in the back of your textbook.

1. I can speak a little Chinese, but (I) speak it not too well.

2. She only knows English, she can't speak other languages.

3. I recognize about two hundred Chinese characters; some I can write, others I can't.

4. He used to be able to write Chinese characters, but now he has completely forgotten.

5. Oh, your Chinese characters are written not badly! (indicate this is something obvious)

Unit 7, Part 3: Translation Exercise

NAME_____ COURSE _____ DATE _____

Translate the following sentences into Pinyin romanization with correct tone marks. If you have forgotten a word, consult the English-Chinese Glossary in the back of your textbook.

1. No wonder the things here are so expensive!

2. I didn't come alone. I came together with my parents.

3. We arrived this year in September. When did you arrive?

4. Sometimes I go with my classmates, sometimes I go alone.

5. My Chinese in the beginning was learned in America, later I studied for a while in China.

· ·

Unit 7, Part 4: Translation Exercise

NAME_____   COURSE _____   DATE _____

Translate the following sentences into Pinyin romanization with correct tone marks. If you have forgotten a word consult the English-Chinese Glossary in the back of your textbook.

1. I hear you speak English very well.

2. Six months ago I couldn't yet speak Chinese.

3. Little Gao, where did you study before you came here?

4. In 3 months, we're going to China for study abroad. ("in 3 months" = "after 3 months")

5. In China the great majority of people start working after they graduate from high school.

Unit 8, Part 1: Translation Exercise

NAME_____   COURSE _____   DATE _____

Translate the following sentences into Pinyin romanization with correct tone marks. If you have forgotten a word, consult the English-Chinese Glossary in the back of your textbook.

1. My home is close to her home.

2. Is your dormitory far from the dining hall?

3. Excuse me, how do you get to Tiananmen?

4. If you take a train, it will probably take more or less two hours.

5. Please keep going straight ahead; when you've passed the Beijing Hotel then you'll have arrived.

· ·

Unit 8, Part 2: Translation Exercise

NAME_____   COURSE _____   DATE _____

Translate the following sentences into Pinyin romanization with correct tone marks. If you have forgotten a wo
consult the English-Chinese Glossary in the back of your textbook.

1. I want a cab to go to the Great Wall Hotel.

2. The car will be there in twenty-five minutes.

3. I have a foreign friend whose last name is Tachelzik.

4. Why don't you wait at the entrance to Capital Airport.

5. Her English name is Mary Smith. She doesn't yet have a Chinese name.

Unit 8, Part 3: Translation Exercise

NAME_____ COURSE _____ DATE _____

Translate the following sentences into Pinyin romanization with correct tone marks. If you have forgotten a word, consult the English-Chinese Glossary in the back of your textbook.

1. How come you still haven't decided what you want to do?

2. At that time it's rush hour; traffic is comparatively congested.

3. Could I trouble you to be a little faster, all right? Soon we'll be late!

4. They said the car had already been dispatched and would be there in twenty minutes.

5. I called you on the phone an hour ago to ask for a taxi. (don't use **zhōngtóu** for "hour")

Unit 8, Part 4: Translation Exercise

NAME_____ COURSE _____ DATE _____

Translate the following sentences into Pinyin romanization with correct tone marks. If you have forgotten a wo
consult the English-Chinese Glossary in the back of your textbook.

1. Those three pieces of luggage are all mine.

2. A: How much do you weigh? B: I weigh 62 kilos.

3. How much time does one need from here to the airport?

4. A: How tall is she? B: It seems she's about one meter seventy.

5. There's a traffic jam here again; we have no choice but to change to a different road.

Unit 9, Part 1: Translation Exercise

NAME_____ COURSE_____ DATE_____

Translate the following sentences into Pinyin romanization with correct tone marks. If you have forgotten a word, consult the English-Chinese Glossary in the back of your textbook.

1. Ask her what colors she likes.

2. Turn right at the next intersection.

3. When you pass the third traffic light, turn east.

4. My daughter likes blue and yellow; my son likes black and white.

5. He isn't a person from this locality; he's probably not very clear either.

· ·

Unit 9, Part 2: Translation Exercise

NAME_____ COURSE _____ DATE _____

Translate the following sentences into Pinyin romanization with correct tone marks. If you have forgotten a wo
consult the English-Chinese Glossary in the back of your textbook.

1. Excuse me, to get to the zoo, what bus number do you take?

2. The zoo? I have to think for a second; I'm not too clear either.

3. You first take bus number 578; then transfer to street car number 232.

4. The street car has come. Get on quickly! You don't need to wait for me.

5. We keep many small animals at our house: cats, dogs, fish, and birds, we have them all!

Unit 9, Part 3: Translation Exercise

NAME_____ COURSE _____ DATE _____

Translate the following sentences into Pinyin romanization with correct tone marks. If you have forgotten a word, consult the English-Chinese Glossary in the back of your textbook.

1. I just got on. When did you get on?

2. Your room is not only clean, but it's also very neat.

3. I'll pay; you don't need to pay. ("pay" = "give money")

4. The students there, some are hard-working, some are lazy.

5. Two tickets to Tiananmen. When we get to Tiananmen, please call me.

· ·

Unit 9, Part 4: Translation Exercise

NAME_____   COURSE _____   DATE _____

Translate the following sentences into Pinyin romanization with correct tone marks. If you have forgotten a wo[r]
consult the English-Chinese Glossary in the back of your textbook.

1. I'm not sleepy; I can't fall asleep. Do you think you can fall asleep?

2. I can understand spoken Chinese, but I can't read Chinese characters.

3. A: I suppose we'll soon be there? B: It's still early, there are still three stations.

4. Never mind, I remember he bought a ticket. In the future he should be more careful!

5. I'm sorry, my classmate bought a ticket but now he can't find it. What should be done?

. . . .

Unit 10, Part 1: Translation Exercise

NAME_____ COURSE _____ DATE _____

Translate the following sentences into Pinyin romanization with correct tone marks. If you have forgotten a word, consult the English-Chinese Glossary in the back of your textbook.

1. The weather report says that starting Friday, it's going to get hotter and hotter.

2. Tomorrow the high temperature is 37 degrees, the low temperature is 28 degrees.

3. This morning is cloudy; this afternoon it's possible it will change to clear weather.

4. Dang it, it's started raining; now it has thundered. Do you think lightning will strike?

5. Don't ask her; she's merely a child, she doesn't necessarily know either. (use zhǐ...éryǐ)

. . . .

Unit 10, Part 2: Translation Exercise

NAME_____   COURSE _____   DATE _____

Translate the following sentences into Pinyin romanization with correct tone marks. If you have forgotten a wo
consult the English-Chinese Glossary in the back of your textbook.

1. Today is a cloudy day; if the sun came out, then it would be good.

2. The season I like the most is spring, so I've come at just the right time!

3. Hey, the weather here is not bad. Neither cold nor hot, quite comfortable.

4. If you want to have a good time in Canada, summer is the most appropriate.

5. In the winter it's extremely cold; in the summer it's both dry and hot, and it seldom rains.

Unit 10, Part 3: Translation Exercise

NAME_____   COURSE _____   DATE _____

Translate the following sentences into Pinyin romanization with correct tone marks. If you have forgotten a word, consult the English-Chinese Glossary in the back of your textbook.

1. What are you doing? Don't go in! Come out quickly!

2. We encountered a big typhoon; we really had bad luck.

3. Taiwan is both hot and humid; in the winter it often drizzles.

4. Recently it's been raining every day, there's no way at all to go outdoors.

5. Actually, it's snowing right now, but because it's too far away, you can't tell.

Unit 10, Part 4: Translation Exercise

NAME_____   COURSE _____   DATE _____

Translate the following sentences into Pinyin romanization with correct tone marks. If you have forgotten a wo consult the English-Chinese Glossary in the back of your textbook.

1. The East Coast of the U.S. is not as dry as the West Coast.

2. Where in China is your home? What is the climate like there?

3. When I first arrived, I didn't adapt too well; later it was pretty much O.K.

4. I feel that the scenery on the West Coast is more beautiful than on the East Coast.

5. The winters here are warmer than New York, and the summers are cooler than New York.

Translation Exercises, Units 1–10: For Each Complete Unit

Unit 1: Translation Exercise

NAME _____ COURSE _____ DATE _____

Translate the following sentences into Pinyin romanization with correct tone marks. If you have forgotten a word, consult the English-Chinese Glossary in the back of your textbook.

1. Mr. Zhao is a good teacher; he is very interesting.

2. Chinese is not too hard, and it's also not too easy.

3. Miss Ke, welcome! Please come in, please sit down.

4. Mrs. Li, has your work been busy recently? (be polite)

5. I'm going to take care of some things. How about you?

6. She is very tall; her mom and dad are also both very tall.

7. I'll go to the library; you please go back to the dormitory.

8. We have all gotten tired. Have you (plural) **also gotten tired?**

9. I have a little something to do; I must be going now. Goodbye!

10. Little Lin, how are you? Long time no see! Where are you going?

....

Unit 2: Translation Exercise

NAME_____ COURSE _____ DATE _____

Translate the following sentences into Pinyin romanization with correct tone marks. If you have forgotten a wo
consult the English-Chinese Glossary in the back of your textbook.

1. I know Ms. Ma from the U.S. Embassy.

2. I suppose your studies must be very intense.

3. General Manager He, welcome to America! (be polite)

4. A: Sorry, I got it wrong, I didn't bring name cards. B: Never mind.

5. Excuse me, who is that? What's his name? What unit does he work in?

6. Don't address me like that. It would be better if you called me Little Wu.

7. My mother and I work at a trading company, my dad doesn't work anymore.

8. I will introduce you: this gentleman is my new colleague; his last name is Bai.

9. Old Wang, don't go back to the dining hall. It would be better if you went to the library.

10. They're my classmates; they're not all Americans. Little Lin is Chinese; she's very busy.

Unit 3: Translation Exercise

NAME_____ COURSE _____ DATE _____

Translate the following sentences into Pinyin romanization with correct tone marks. If you have forgotten a word, consult the English-Chinese Glossary in the back of your textbook.

1. How much is nine plus eight minus six?

2. This bag is cheap. Why don't you buy one too?

3. I don't have an older brother, also don't have an older sister.

4. In our Chinese class, in all there are twelve classmates, right?

5. This one costs $4,000, that one costs $5,000. Too expensive!

6. Would it be all right if I took a look at your name card? Thanks!

7. I'm afraid the classmate who works in the library is no longer coming.

8. Let me try to think... My mom will be forty-seven years old next month.

9. My mom and dad are coming at 11:45; it will still take an hour and a half.

10. A: How much does that cup cost? B: This cup only costs two dollars and ninety-eight cents.

. . . .

Unit 4: Translation Exercise

NAME_____   COURSE _____   DATE _____

Translate the following sentences into Pinyin romanization with correct tone marks. If you have forgotten a wo
consult the English-Chinese Glossary in the back of your textbook.

1. She was born in Taipei on July 23, 1995.

2. This is the third time that he's going to China.

3. It seems Hong Kong has more than seven million people.

4. It seems yesterday was October 17, a Wednesday. Is that right?

5. This is my second time here; this time I'm going to stay for three months.

6. That trading company is open half-days on Saturdays; it's closed on Sundays.

7. The library opens daily at 8:45 in the morning and closes at 7:30 in the evening.

8. I've been to Shanghai, but I've never been to Guangzhou. Have you been there?

9. The first person wants to go for one day; the second person wants to go for one year.

10. Her address is 6th Floor, No. 108, Alley 22, Lane 345, Nanjing East Road Section Three.

Unit 5: Translation Exercise

NAME_____   COURSE _____   DATE _____

Translate the following sentences into Pinyin romanization with correct tone marks. If you have forgotten a word, consult the English-Chinese Glossary in the back of your textbook.

1. If you're tired, you may sleep here.

2. Little Sun, do you know where the boss is?

3. Miss Zhang was not in. I left her a message.

4. Is she also studying Chinese at Peking University?

5. Last year they moved to Tianjin; it's east of Beijing.

6. Next month Mrs. Chen is coming here to study English.

7. The dog was on the bookshelf, the child was under the table.

8. This computer is a little cheaper, that computer is a little more expensive.

9. It will soon be 12:00. The shoe factory workers will soon be eating lunch.

10. A: Where does Mr. Bai live? B: He lives in Nanjing, to the west of Shanghai.

· ·

Unit 6: Translation Exercise

NAME_____ COURSE _____ DATE _____

Translate the following sentences into Pinyin romanization with correct tone marks. If you have forgotten a word, consult the English-Chinese Glossary in the back of your textbook.

1. I'm a first-year and she's a junior. What year are you in?

2. My friend was born in China and then grew up in America.

3. Mrs. Zheng, this is a little present which we are giving you.

4. A: How old is her son? B: He's still small. It seems he's seven months old.

5. She's already over 70, but because she eats lots of good things, she looks young.

6. A: Are you married? B: My older brother is already married; I'm not yet married.

7. That Chinese person said that American food looks good but does not taste very good.

8. I have one older sister, she works at Southwest Airlines. Do you have brothers or sisters?

9. Sorry, I forgot to introduce myself. My surname is Huang. I'm a teacher; I teach junior high.

10. A: I suppose your daughter is already in elementary school? B: Yes, she's already in second grade.

Unit 7: Translation Exercise

NAME_____   COURSE_____   DATE_____

Translate the following sentences into Pinyin romanization with correct tone marks. If you have forgotten a word, consult the English-Chinese Glossary in the back of your textbook.

1. Where did you live before coming to America?

2. You say you have one child, right? A boy or a girl? How old?

3. I've heard that Little Chen knows German, French, and Japanese.

4. A: Did you go by yourself? B: No, I went together with three classmates.

5. A: Can you write Chinese? B: I can write a little, but I don't write it very well.

6. Do you know if that American teacher can speak Standard Chinese (Mandarin)?

7. She lived in Spain for over eleven years. No wonder she speaks Spanish so well.

8. After graduating from high school, she worked for two years, then she applied to college.

9. The Chinese University of Hong Kong has several thousand students. Some I know, others I don't.

10. A: You speak English very well, you know! Where did you learn it? B: I learned it in kindergarten.

. . . .

Unit 8: Translation Exercise

NAME_____ COURSE _____ DATE _____

Translate the following sentences into Pinyin romanization with correct tone marks. If you have forgotten a word, consult the English-Chinese Glossary in the back of your textbook.

1. Excuse me, how do I get to Taiwan University?

2. We'll come looking for you in half an hour, O.K.?

3. It seems that my home is not very far from your home.

4. Miss Li is not at her desk. Please call her again in ten minutes.

5. The tourists who come from America almost all stay at the Beijing Hotel.

6. These two pieces of luggage are mine, those three pieces of luggage are his.

7. Don't get excited, I think Professor Wang is likely to come in just a little while.

8. Keep going straight, after you've passed the French Embassy you then will have arrived.

9. A: How long does it take to get from there to the foreign ministry? B: One hour, more or less.

10. Darn it, I forgot! New Asia Trading Co. is closed today. We have no choice but to come again tomorrow.

Unit 9: Translation Exercise

NAME_____ COURSE _____ DATE _____

Translate the following sentences into Pinyin romanization with correct tone marks. If you have forgotten a word, consult the English-Chinese Glossary in the back of your textbook.

1. He's not only stupid but also lazy.

2. First take the bus, then take the trolley.

3. When we get to Tiananmen, please call me.

4. She likes red and blue. What colors do you like?

5. I can't fall asleep on trains. Can you fall asleep on trains?

6. Go straight from here and turn left at the first traffic light.

7. You don't need to ask her, she's not very clear about it either.

8. First turn to the east, then turn to the west, and you'll be there!

9. I'm sorry, I can't find my name cards. (don't use **kéyi** or **néng**)

10. At home we raise fish. Do you keep any small animals at home?

. . . .

Unit 10: Translation Exercise

NAME_____   COURSE _____   DATE _____

Translate the following sentences into Pinyin romanization with correct tone marks. If you have forgotten a word, consult the English-Chinese Glossary in the back of your textbook.

1. When Old Wang died, everybody was very sad.

2. The east coast of the U.S. is not as dry as the west coast.

3. This winter I'm going to Beijing. Is Beijing colder than New York?

4. I'm playing with my computer; Old Sun is sleeping. What are you doing?

5. Macao is hot every day—both hot and humid, so we seldom go outdoors.

6. Recently the weather has been cooler and cooler, more and more comfortable.

7. Starting tomorrow, I'm going to be working at the embassy. I'm so nervous I'm going to die.

8. The weather forecast said that tomorrow the high temperature will be 33° and the low temperature 25°.

9. If it rains tomorrow, then we won't go out to have fun; but the weather report isn't necessarily accurate.

10. A: My friends are neither many nor few. B: I have only one good friend. C: I don't have friends at all.

Cornelius C. Kubler is Stanfield Professor of Asian Studies at Williams College, where he teaches Chinese and for many years chaired the Department of Asian Studies. He was formerly Chinese Language Training Supervisor and Chair of the Department of Asian and African Languages at the Foreign Service Institute, U.S. Department of State, where he trained American diplomats in Chinese and other languages, and he served for six years as Principal of the American Institute in Taiwan Chinese Language & Area Studies School. Kubler, who has directed intensive Chinese language training programs in the U.S., mainland China, and Taiwan, has been active in Chinese language test development and has authored or coauthored nine books and over 50 articles on Chinese language pedagogy and linguistics.

Yang Wang, native to Beijing, is a Lecturer in Chinese at Brown University, where she teaches all levels of modern Chinese language. Before joining the Brown faculty, she taught Chinese at The Ohio State University and Williams College. She also taught for several years at the Middlebury College Summer Chinese School. Wang is interested in the implications of pragmatics in Chinese pedagogical practice, teaching materials development, and the integration of technology into the curriculum.